Not Another Apple for the TEACHER

Not Another Apple for the TEACHER

Hundreds of Fascinating Facts from the World of Education

Erin Barrett and
Jack Mingo

METRO BOOKS
NEW YORK

This 2010 edition published by Metro Books,
by arrangement with Red Wheel/Weiser,llc.

Cover Illustration: Colin Johnson
Cover and Book Design: Claudia Smelser
Author Photo: Jen Fariello

Metro Books
122 Fifth Avenue
New York, NY 10011

ISBN: 978-1-4351-2402-8

Printed and bound in the United States of America
1 3 5 7 9 10 8 6 4 2

Not Another Apple for the TEACHER!

	A Word from the Authors	vii
ONE	Out of the Halls and into the Classroom	1
TWO	Don't Know Much about History	17
THREE	First in Its Class	37
FOUR	Where the Word Things Are	45
FIVE	Past Lives	55
SIX	Before They Were Famous	75
SEVEN	Tools of the Trade	95
EIGHT	Teacher Appreciation	125
NINE	Fightin' Words	139
TEN	Teaching by the Numbers	145
ELEVEN	Educational Follies	157
TWELVE	Life on Campus	175
THIRTEEN	Worldly Wise	193
FOURTEEN	The Wild World of School Sports	197

FIFTEEN	Truer Words Were Never Spoken	209
SIXTEEN	Teachers on Page, Stage, and Screen	219
SEVENTEEN	An Alternative Education	227
EIGHTEEN	Lunches, Libraries, and Bus Drivers	231
	Acknowledgments	239
	Selected References	241
	About the Authors	245

A Word from the Authors

"In the first place, God made idiots. That was for practice. Then he made school boards."

—Mark Twain

Beware, dear reader. This is not your typical book about teachers. If you're looking for a sickly sweet, sentimental book, put this one down right now and pick up the one with the inspirational sayings and the big shiny apple on the cover.

This is a book for teachers who think and laugh, and for the people who love them. Instead of sweet platitudes, it's a book of fun, odd, illuminating, and sometimes sad facts—the good and bad, the triumphs and foibles—about the world of education.

Did you know, for example, that the classic school desk was based on the desks used by monks during the Middle Ages? That 2,500 years ago, the Chinese philosopher Confucius was the first to advocate public schools for all? That the

Hebrew word *musar* means both "education" and "corporal punishment"? Did you know that New Jersey has a law on the books that requires that schoolchildren be taught about the Irish potato famine? That a hundred years ago, the math-impaired Kansas legislature passed a law saying that π could legally be rounded down to 3?

Well, you get the idea.

And, by the way, we learned some things in the course of researching this book. Here's one of them: Despite public misconception, teachers don't particularly like apples. You can't believe how many are showered with scores of apple tchotchkes—apples, apple mugs, apple rulers, apple paperweights, apple picture frames, apple pens, apple sweaters, and more. In fact, the overwhelming message we got from teachers was, "No more apples!" We don't blame them—such a deluge could turn even Johnny Appleseed into an apple-hater.

So listen up, everybody: Teachers are tired of being seen as one-dimensional apple-munching cardboard figures. We can safely say that any teacher will love this book, especially if the alternative is an apple.

However, let's not stop there. Let us assure you that you don't have to be a teacher to love these fun and informative facts. In fact, your assignment is to buy this book and read it. Better do it today, because we can't promise that there won't be a pop quiz first thing tomorrow.

Erin Barrett
Jack Mingo

one

Out of the Halls and into the Classroom

"Life is like high school with money."

—*Frank Zappa*

During the days of the one-room schoolhouse, teachers were normally offered room and board on a rotating basis at the homes of their students; male teachers were often threatened, beaten, and run out of town for sport by older boys who didn't want to be in class. Classes could include as many as forty students of all ages, with older students often recruited to teach the younger ones.

Teachers in the 1800s used to use tongue twisters to teach articulation. Read along with some of these vintage lessons:

Some shun sunshine. Do you shun sunshine?
The big black bear bled blood.
The sixth sheik's sixth sheep's sick.

Three gray geese sat on the green grass grazing.
She's so selfish she should sell shellfish shells.
Sheep shouldn't sleep in a shack.
One old Oxford ox opening oysters.
The skunk thunk the stump stunk.

"**I** see the mind of a five-year-old as a volcano with two vents: destructiveness and creativeness."

—Sylvia Ashton-Warner

"**T**he fellow in charge of Sumerian language studies said 'Why didn't you speak Sumerian?' and caned me. My teacher said: 'Your handwriting is unsatisfactory' and caned me. I began to hate the scribal arts."

—Mesopotamian student, circa 1700 B.C.E., found on a clay tablet in Nippur, Iraq

The Hebrew word *musar* means both "education" and "corporal punishment."

The classic school desk, with a sloping top and a storage space below, is based on the work desks used by monks during the Middle Ages for transcribing and illuminating manuscripts.

Not Another Apple!

"An apple is an excellent thing—until you have tried a peach."

—George du Maurier (1834–1896)

Giving an apple to the teacher as a symbolic gesture came from a time when

American teachers were often paid in farm goods by cash-poor townspeople. It wasn't easy to be a teacher—many had to take after-hours jobs as choir leaders, grave-diggers, or bartenders in order to earn a decent living.

According to a recent national poll, students and their parents gave 26,367,513 apple-related gifts to teachers last year. Of these gifts, nearly a third (8,076,028) were real apples—the rest (18,291,485) were apple-themed tchotchkes—coffee mugs, paperweights, picture frames, stationery, fridge magnets, and others.

The average K–12 teacher gets 7.06 apple-related gifts per year: 2.16 actual apples and 4.9 apple-themed decorations.

Elementary school teachers get nearly twice as many apple gifts as middle school teachers and more than five times as many as high school teachers.

The highest number of apples received by one teacher last year? That record probably goes to fifth-grade teacher Paul Kueffner of Cider Mill School in Wilton, Connecticut. To teach his kids about the old cider mill that gave his school its name, Kueffner convinced his PTA to buy a small cider press. His students gave him 2,200 apples.

Kueffner was unusual in that he actually asked for apple gifts. Most teachers become ambivalent about them over time. One respondent amassed a collection of more than a thousand apple knickknacks over a long career. Most, however, said they'd prefer almost anything to another apple gift.

What did teachers in the poll say they'd like instead? Books, "a smile from a student," teaching supplies, an appreciative note, student photos, candles, gift certificates for movies, massages, and restaurants, "chew toys for my dog," flowers, chocolate, coffee, "a good red wine (preferably Bordeaux)," money, whiskey, "plane tickets to exotic locations," and "a millionaire."

Of all the farm goods once given to teachers, why has it become "an *apple* for the teacher" instead of an egg, a tomato, a sack of wheat, or a hamhock? After extensive research, we can say with relative certainty that nobody seems to know. Here are some educated guesses:

- Apples are cheap and can be eaten without any preparation. They can also be given in the morning without going bad by the end of the school day (as opposed to, say, "a quart of milk for the teacher").
- Students are wishing teachers good health, as in the apple a day that keeps doctors away.
- Apples and education are linked in the public mind because of a Bible story. An apple is what granted Adam and Eve knowledge to discern good from evil. Unfortunately, that knowledge also got them expelled from the Garden of Eden. The disturbing thing about this interpretation is that it implies a comparison between a teacher and the snake that forever ruined humanity's innocent happiness on Earth. Such a thought, of course, is completely preposterous.

"Examinations are formidable even to the best prepared, for the greatest fool may ask more than the wisest man can answer."

—*C. C. Colton*

They don't name textbooks like they used to. If you were in a nineteenth-century classroom, you might find yourself teaching from a book called *The English Reader, Or Pieces in Prose and Poetry: Selected From the Best Writers: Designed to Assist Young Persons to Read With Propriety and Effect, to Improve Their Language and Sentiments, and to Inculcate Some of the Most Important Principles of Piety and Virtue: With a Few Preliminary Observations on the Principles of Good Reading,* by one Lindley Murray.

By the time you told your students to get out their textbooks, class would be over. How about: *Osgood's Progressive Fifth Reader: Embracing a System of Instruction in the Principles of Elocution, and Selections for Reading and Speaking From the Best English and American Authors: Designed for the Use of Academies and the Highest Classes in Public and Private Schools,* by Lucius Osgood?

"**T**he secret to speed-reading is moving your lips faster."

—*Charles Schultz*

It's not just a popular stereotype: Most schoolhouses in the 1800s really were painted red. Why was that? Probably for the same reason that barns were—red paint hid dirt easily and was easy to make without having to resort to expensive store-bought paint.

How do you make "Schoolhouse Red" paint? Start with skim milk and mix in some linseed oil and lime for the base. Scrap off the rust from some old farm tools and put it in for the red color. Perfect!

"**N**ature makes boys and girls lovely to look upon so they can be tolerated until they acquire some sense."

—William Lyon Phelps, renowned author and Yale professor (1856–1943)

In 1921, reflective of anti-Cajun prejudice, the state of Louisiana specifically passed laws to prevent any teacher from speaking "Cajun French" in public schools.

O soft! What light on yonder student breaks? The Shakespeare play assigned most often in classrooms is *Romeo and Juliet.*

Both Socrates and Plato thought that reading was a poor way of learning. They believed that a student learned more from a good speaker than from a good writer.

"**O**ne of the disadvantages of having children is that they eventually get old enough to give you presents they make at school."

—Robert Byrne

Jigsaw puzzles got their start not as an outlet for entertainment but as a teaching tool. Originally, eighteenth-century teachers used puzzles to teach geography, and students had to put together states or countries that had been cut out of a map. Puzzles became so popular that they were broadened to teach subjects like zoology and the alphabet as well.

The "Physical Sciences" technically consist of Mathematics, Physics, Astronomy, Chemistry, and Earth Sciences.

If you live in Missouri, you likely know that the state fossil is the crinoid, sometimes called the "sea lily." This odd, plant-like creature inhabited the region millions of years ago, leaving a large quantity of fossils in the state. You may not know, however, that if it weren't for a group of schoolkids in 1989 lobbying and pressuring the Missouri General Assembly, the crinoid might never have gained official status.

Do you remember William Figueroa? Probably not. He was the twelve-year-old who nationally embarrassed Dan Quayle during a spelling bee when he spelled out *potato* without an *e*. "I knew he was wrong, but since he's the vice-president, I went and put an *e* on. Afterward I went to a dictionary and there was potato like I spelled it." Figueroa went on to make money from the experience in commentating, sales, and appearances at places like the Democratic National Convention and the David Letterman show. Quayle never really lived down his gaff.

"He who has imagination but no education has wings but no feet."

—Old French proverb

In the United States, gold is used to make class rings more often than any other piece of jewelry.

In 1990, when preschoolers were polled about who should run for president, Mr. Rogers, of the children's show *Mr. Roger's Neighborhood,* was their first choice. Sometimes the greatest wisdom comes from the youngest among us.

"There must be such a thing as a child with average ability, but you can't find a parent who will admit that it is his child."

—Thomas Bailey, Florida's Superintendent of Schools

A researcher asked kids which season is most boring, and 53 percent said, "Summer." Apparently kids prefer school to just hanging around the house.

two

Don't Know Much about History

It was the written word that made school as we know it possible. Before that, young people had to repeat orally whatever they wanted to learn, and they could learn no more than their teacher had memorized.

In 1500 B.C.E., Semitic tribes developed alphabets that corresponded to vocal sounds, like ours, which made words easier to sound out. Certain Hebrew tribes began teaching reading and writing to everybody in the tribe, not just the affluent—boys in the schools, girls at home—so that all could read the sacred books.

"Learning without thought is labor lost."

—*Confucius*

Confucius practiced what he preached. He wrote that he never refused any sincere student, "even if he came to me on foot, with nothing more to offer as tuition than a package of dried meat."

Unfortunately, there's no evidence that the rest of China followed the sage's example. It wasn't until centuries later that peasant boys were given a guaranteed chance at an education.

Socrates, who died in 399 B.C.E., believed that everybody already has true knowledge within their brain somewhere. His teaching style, asking a series of probing questions, was designed to bring that preexisting knowledge to consciousness.

Socrates' most famous student was Plato. Plato's most famous student was Aristotle. Aristotle's most famous student was Alexander the Great, who used all of that accumulated knowledge to go on a military rampage, conquering pretty much all of the known world.

"The legislator should direct his attention to the education of youth. As a citizen the student should be molded to suit the form of government under which he lives."

—*Aristotle*

Aristotle started a school he called the Lyceum. Everyone else called it the Peripatetic ("Walking Around") School, however, because teachers led discussions while strolling absentmindedly around the grounds.

The Romans took public speaking seriously, more seriously than most other school subjects. Marcus Fabius Quintilianus, a Roman oratory teacher in the '70s and '80s C.E., wrote a famous twelve-volume textbook called *Institutio Oratoria,* for training public speakers from infancy to adulthood.

Compare the educational systems in ancient Athens and Sparta:

- In Athens, all sons of free citizens were given an education.
- However, this was less than universal education, because free citizens made up only about a third of the city's population, and girls were not provided formal education (though many were tutored at home).
- In Sparta, in contrast, boys and girls were both given schooling . . . but unlike Athens'

more rounded curriculum, Sparta's schools taught mostly warrior skills to the boys, and physical education to the girls, to make them healthy mothers of future soldiers.

- Some of the character-building skills taught to Spartan youths included killing, stealing, and successfully deceiving others.

In 100 B.C.E., Rome built the most extensive school system seen up to that time. Their schools were modeled after Athens' liberal arts curriculum, and the schools taught both boys and girls.

Education was so distrusted as "pagan" by the early Christian church that at the beginning of the third century, anyone wanting to teach school was forbidden in the church. Schoolteachers were not even allowed to be baptized.

Julian, Emperor of the Byzantine Empire from 361 to 363 C.E., was the first leader to mandate state examinations for teachers.

Theodosius II, who ruled from 408 to 450 C.E., made it a state offense for any teacher to teach without a state license, and then made sure that the licenses went to people who conformed to the orthodoxy he supported. Not that anything like this could ever happen today, mind you.

Knight school in the Middle Ages was informal and consisted of some reading, writing, and figuring, but also such valuable subjects as lute playing, chess, and chivalry.

In the Middle Ages, Western European education at its basic—or elementary—level was divided into three categories of study collectively called the *Trivium,* consisting of grammar, rhetoric, and logic. Higher grades of education were divided into four categories. These were geometry, astronomy, basic math, and music, collectively called the *Quadrivium.*

In the 1100s, the first modern universities were developed in Europe. There were two models of university that developed about the same time. The University of Paris model, followed in most of Northern Europe, consisted of a guild of teachers who ran the school and recruited students into it. The University of Bologna model, followed in most of Southern Europe, consisted of guilds of students who ran the school, hired the professors, and set their working conditions.

University professors in Europe during the Middle Ages taught their lessons orally, so literacy was not a college prerequisite. In fact, many students decided it was best to put off learning to read and write until after they had gotten college out of the way.

The "dame schools" of England were often the only elementary schools available for village children in the sixteenth and seventeenth centuries. They were run by women who taught out of their homes for a small fee.

Early American colonists followed the "dame school" model. Only about one in ten children went to school—the rest became apprentices.

There probably wouldn't be a network of Catholic parochial schools in the United States if the Protestants in power had been a little more tolerant (or kept religion out of the schools completely). From 1830 to 1850 a million Catholics, many from Ireland, immigrated to the eastern seaboard. They were the target of suspicion and prejudice from the Protestants already living there, who passed laws to ensure that the public schools used the King James Bible, Protestant prayers, and Protestant interpretations of God and scriptures.

The Maine Supreme Court ruled that a school board had the constitutional right to expel a Catholic or any other child for refusing to read from the assigned version of the Bible. In Philadelphia, the school board agreed to let Catholic children read from the church-approved Douay Bible, but that was met by denunciations from Protestant pulpits, riots, the burning of Catholic churches, and several deaths. Finally, the Catholic hierarchy decided that starting their own schools was the only answer to keeping their children safe and in the faith.

New York had the first state board of education, established in 1794.

Kindergarten seems self-evident now, but it was a hard sell when Friedrich Froebel first suggested it. The idea of encouraging the growth of a child through action and play seemed like a radical idea at the time. In 1851 the Prussian government banned all kindergartens in Prussia—it didn't lift the ban until nine years later.

The Reform Movement of the mid-nineteenth century in America didn't just work for the abolition of slavery and better conditions for prisoners, laborers, and the institutionalized. Reformers also pushed for women's rights and for a free national public education system.

Forty-three educators in Philadelphia founded the National Teachers Association in1857, which later became the National Education Association (NEA), "to elevate the character and advance the interests of the teaching profession, and to promote the cause of popular education in the United States." That's great, but the organization undercut its goals by refusing to grant memberships to women until 1866. It also excluded teachers in private schools.

The NEA now lets almost everyone in, including people whom you wouldn't normally consider educators. For example, while most of its 2.6 million members are teachers, its membership also includes about 68,000 students, 125,000 administrators, guidance counselors, and librarians, and 218,000 school secretaries, teacher aides, cafeteria workers, bus drivers, and custodians.

Massachusetts was the first state to enact a compulsory attendance act in 1852. It required all children except those who were in abject poverty, were disabled, or were already knowledgeable to attend school for at least three months of every year if they were between the ages of eight and fourteen. At least six of the weeks had to be consecutive. Failure for meeting this requirement? The parents were fined not more than $20. It wasn't always effective, but it was a start.

By 1918 all states had a compulsory attendance law of some kind on the books.

Alexander Graham Bell's father was a speech expert; his mother was deaf. These two factors led the inventor to become a teacher of the deaf. It was Bell, based on his own expertise, who suggested that a special teacher should be hired to help young blind and deaf Helen Keller cope with her world.

Where did the Waldorf schools get their name? Not from the hotel nor the salad, at least not directly. It was from the Waldorf-Astoria cigarette company in Germany (which, to give it some class, was named after the famous New York hotel—which in turn was named after its owner Waldorf Astor, but that's another story). The owner of the cigarette company, Emil Molt, wanted to give the children of his factory workers a good education. He commissioned educator Rudolf Steiner to invent a school that would encourage individuals to live in freedom and personal integrity, and funded a prototype. The Waldorf school model quickly spread worldwide, and the first North American opened in Manhattan . . . ironically, not far from the Waldorf-Astoria Hotel.

The last time that American education went through a test-'em-to-death fad was early in the twentieth century. From that testing mania we got IQ tests and the Stanford-Binet Intelligence Test . . . but we also got tests that purported to measure a child's intelligence and learning by the size and shape of the student's head.

Adults in pre-mass media America were so hungry for intellectual stimulation that traveling lecturers on serious subjects could attract standing-room-only crowds. Called "Chautauquas" after the New York camp where the idea began, over a million people in 10,000 towns across America attended lectures on politics, the arts, and contemporary issues in 1924 alone.

Blue Cross and Blue Shield, the insurance company, was originally created in 1929 for schoolteachers, to give them, if necessary, three weeks of hospital care a year for an annual fee of $6.

President Lyndon Johnson, like his mother before him, was a trained teacher. As a matter of fact, he graduated, class of 1930, from Southwest State Teachers College San Marcos, Texas. And in order to pay for his education he taught elementary school in Cotulla, Texas, for a year. After his graduation, he went on to teach speech classes at the high school level.

You'd think there'd be more school districts now than in the past, but that's not true. Smaller districts consolidated into bigger ones. In 1940 there were more than 117,000 school districts—fifty years later, there were barely 15,000.

Its real name is the "Servicemen's Readjustment Act of 1944," but you probably know it by its nickname, the "GI Bill."

How things have changed: In 1960, when Janet Reno entered Harvard Law School, there were only fifteen other women studying there. Now, the average law school class is about one-half female.

When the miniskirt first came into style in the 1960s, most public schools in America required that the hem of a girl's skirt touch the floor when she is kneeling. If it didn't, the skirt was officially considered a miniskirt, and the student was sent home.

Outside government or military affairs, the Internet as we know it was originally a link among the University of Utah, the Stanford Research Institute, and the University of California-Los Angeles and the University of California-Santa Barbara.

Low on the totem pole: In the line of succession for U.S. president the Secretary of Education is way down at the bottom of a long list. Succession is as follows: Vice President, Speaker of the House,

President Pro Tempore of the Senate, Secretary of State, Secretary of Treasury, Secretary of Defense, Attorney General, Secretary of the Interior, Secretary of Agriculture, Secretaries of Commerce, Labor, Health and Human Services, Housing and Urban Development, Transportation, and Energy. If all of those die or are incapacitated, then the presidency goes to the Secretary of Education. The only position below the Secretary of Education's slot is the Secretary of Veterans' Affairs. The cabinet members are lined up according to when their offices were created.

three

First in Its Class

The Sumerians first wrote in cuneiform in 3500 B.C.E.; the Egyptians began writing with pictographs in 3000 B.C.E. Both developed schools in about 3000 B.C.E. to teach the rather difficult art of writing, and only a small, specialized class of scribes and their sons were able to attend.

The Chinese teacher and philosopher Confucius (551–479 B.C.E.) may have been the first to advocate public schools that were open to all. "In education there should be no class distinctions," he wrote. "Even a peasant boy can become a man of intellect and principle."

The Chinese wrote the first encyclopedia in 220 B.C.E. It was called *The Emperor's Mirror* and included history, biographies, and literature. No copies have survived, alas.

The first college in America was Harvard, chartered in 1636 as "a schoale or colledge" by the Massachusetts General Court.

Benjamin Franklin opened the first public library in America. That was in 1731.

The first school to teach only law opened its doors in 1774 in Litchfield, Connecticut. It closed them for good in 1833.

The oldest school fraternity? Phi Beta Kappa was the first, organized in 1776 at William & Mary College. Although it later changed from a general fraternity to an honors society, it started the trend among its imitators of using Greek letters for names. It takes its name from the initial letters of its motto, *Philosophia biou kubernetes* ("Philosophy is the guide of life").

Here's someone to blame when you have to wake up early for school: Levi Hutchens of Concord, New Hampshire. He's the guy who, in 1787, invented the first alarm clock.

The first state university to open in North America was the University of North Carolina at Chapel Hill. Although it was founded in 1789, it didn't begin enrolling students until 1795.

The first academy to devote its curriculum solely to educating teachers was the Concord Academy in Vermont. The Reverend Samuel Read Hall opened the academy doors in 1823.

The first coeducational college in the United States? The Oberlin Collegiate

Institute (now Oberlin College) integrated men with women in 1833.

In 1873, St. Louis became home to the first public kindergarten in the United States.

The first private kindergarten was begun twenty-three years earlier in Watertown, Wisconsin. Its founder, Margaretha Schurz, had been a pupil of Friedrich Froebel, who started the kindergarten movement in 1837. *Kindergarten,* by the way, is German for "children's garden." It was Froebel's second choice for a name. His first choice had been *kleinkender-beschaftigungsanstalt,* which means "institution where small children are occupied," but even Germans had trouble saying it. . . .

The first person over Niagara Falls in a barrel was Annie Taylor, a schoolteacher from Bay City, Michigan, on October 24, 1901. She survived, but, bruised and battered, her advice after emerging from the barrel was, "No one ought ever do that again." Taylor rode the wave of her successful feat for a while, but later died in poverty.

The first blind and deaf person to graduate from college is exactly who you'd think it was. She accomplished this in 1904. She was, of course, Helen Keller.

The world's first school of journalism opened in 1908 at the University of Missouri at Columbia.

Ella Flagg Young was the first female superintendent of schools for a major city (assuming, of course, that you consider Chicago a major city). She served from 1909 to 1915. Her chief contribution was to introduce practical studies like home economics and manual training.

All right you couch potatoes, do you know what the very first televised sports event was? It was a baseball game broadcast between Ushigome and Awazi Shichiku Higher Elementary Schools on the Tozuka (Japan) Baseball Grounds. The date was September 27, 1931, a day that will live in infamy.

State College High School in State College, Pennsylvania: Besides having a distinctly confusing name, it has the honor of having offered the world's first driver's training course. On February 17, 1934, the first group of sixteen-year-olds shuffled sullenly into the class, hoping to drive the family Model A and raise their parents' insurance rates.

The first Hollywood movie about school violence was *The Blackboard Jungle* (1955).

When in 1962 James Meredith became the first African American to attend the University of Mississippi, huge numbers of students and residents rioted. One hundred and sixty U.S. marshals were wounded (twenty-eight of them by gunfire), and two bystanders were killed.

Although it seems like just 1, 2, 3, 4, 5, 6, 7, 8, 9, or 10 years ago, the first *Sesame Street* was broadcast on November 10, 1969.

four

Where the Word Things Are

The word *school* derives from the Greek *skhole,* which means "leisure." It came from a time when only the children of the idle rich had time to devote to study.

S*cholionophobia* is an unreasonable fear and loathing of school.

Why are principals called that? Before they became solely administrators, the title (and job description) was "principal teacher."

Who or what was the "Montessori" in Montessori schools? Educator Marie Montessori, (1870–1952), who was also the first woman in Italy to earn a medical degree and practice medicine.

University comes from *universitas,* the Latin word for the universe or society.

Drop-out came from a term used in factories for a scrap or a defective product that had to be discarded from the assembly line.

You're walking peacefully in the woods and suddenly flash back to the classroom because someone's calling out, "Teacher!" Maybe it's the teacher bird. Also known as the ovenbird, the teacher is a common American warbler with a brownish green back, dull orange head, and a white breast spotted with black. It got its name because its song sounds like "Teacher! Teacher! *Teacher!*" repeated with increasing loudness.

They're called "liberal arts" not because of political progressivism, but because of the liberation they were meant to give the intellect.

The word *epicurian*—referring to the pleasures of eating and drinking—comes from an ancient schoolteacher named Epicurus. Born in Greece in 341 B.C.E., Epicurus established a school in Athens that tried to teach the pleasures of simplicity and tranquility. Food was just a small part of the philosophy, but the school became nicknamed "the Garden School" and became known as a place for foodies because students provided their own food by growing their own gardens.

Where does the word *pupil* for "student" come from? Not from the part of the eye, but from the Latin word *pupillus,* meaning "small boy." (Strangely enough, the pupil of the eye gets its name from the Latin *pupilla,* meaning "small girl"—called that because of tiny reflections of people seen therein.)

Teach comes from the same root word as *token:* The Old English word *tacn,* meaning "symbol" and "to show."

Why is a second-year student called a sophomore? From *sophism,* the Greek meaning "becoming wise," and the English word *more.* At Cambridge, England, in the 1600s, where the term originated, there were "Fresh Men, Sophy Moores, Sophesters or Junior Sophs, and Senior Sophs," as a writer put it at the time.

Pedagogue came from the Greek meaning "child" and "to lead." The first pedagogues were slaves in Greece and Rome who taught the children of the free men.

The Latin *inter* and *legere* are the root words for the word "intelligence." They mean respectively "between" and "to pick" or "to choose," implying the original meaning of intelligence was the ability to choose between one thing and another.

Why is it called grammar school? The earliest grammar schools strictly taught grammar. But the grammar they taught was not English, but Latin. Eventually, the schools expanded their curriculum; later still, that curriculum and the grammar school name were incorporated into nineteenth-century American public schools.

Classy Words

By poll, American speech teachers came up with a list of the ugliest-sounding words in the English language. See if you agree with their choices. The list included:

plump
gripe
sap
jazz
crunch
treachery
cacophony
phlegmatic
plutocrat
flatulence

What's in a Name? Money, Mostly

Tobacco tycoon James Duke gave Trinity College $107 million in 1925. Shortly after, the college administration decided that "Duke University" had a nice ring to it, and that's what it's called today.

Asa T. Soule of Rochester, New York, had a similar idea. He was the inventor of a very popular, alcohol-heavy patent medicine called Hops Bitters. He offered the regents of University of Rochester

$100,000 if they would change the school's name to Hops Bitters University. The regents said, "No thanks."

Dartmouth College started out as "More's Indian Charity School" in Lebanon, Connecticut. However, the school had trouble finding Native Americans to fill the school, so its founder moved the school to Hanover, New Hampshire, and renamed it after his friend, William Legge—the Earl of Dartmouth—who became the school's major benefactor.

Harvard was named after a thirty-one-year-old British clergyman named John Harvard, who arrived in America in 1638 and died almost immediately afterward.

Still, he lived long enough to write a will, and in that will he left his 400-volume library and £800 sterling to the struggling young college. This won him the college's undying gratitude and his name on the door.

The little town of New Town, Massachusetts, home to the newly christened Harvard, got into the name-changing spirit shortly after the college was founded. It decided to name itself "Cambridge" after England's most famous college town, hoping that some of the old country's magic might rub off.

five

Past Lives

Here's another good reason to keep extensive notes. Only small fragments of Aristotle's writings still exist. His high reputation is based almost completely on his class lecture notes, which somehow survived through the years. In them, he painstakingly and brilliantly outlined his courses on nearly every branch of knowledge and the arts.

"There is nothing in the intellect that was not first perceived in the senses."

—Aristotle

Besides *Paradise Lost, Doctrine and Discipline of Divorce,* and *On the Death of a Fair Infant Dying of a Cough,* writer John Milton also wrote *A Tractate of Education,* a Plato's *Republic*-like book dealing with the education of the young in literature, poetry, and science.

Public education trailblazer Horace Mann retired from a law practice to become Massachusetts' first Secretary of Education in 1837. Mann himself had received only erratic schooling in his childhood, consisting of 8–10 weeks a year. Luckily, he educated himself by reading extensively from the local public library.

Braille, the raised-dot system of reading and writing for the blind, was invented by a teacher. Louis Braille (1809–1852) was himself blind from a serious infection suffered at age three. He entered the Royal Institution for Blind Youth in Paris and stayed to become a teacher. During his tenure, he developed the system of reading that bears his name.

George Boole (1815–1864) invented Boolean algebra. The mathematical theories of logic and probabilities are founded on his writings works. In 1849, he became professor of mathematics at Queen's College, Cork, Ireland. Not bad, considering that he didn't have even a college degree.

William Randolph Hearst's mother, Phoebe, was a Missouri schoolteacher prior to marrying her rich husband. Because of her early experience in education, she became one of the founding members of what would become the PTA and served as the organization's first vice president.

President James Garfield was a college professor and (at age twenty-six) president of the Western Reserve Eclectic Institute (now Hiram College) in Hiram, Ohio.

Caroline Scott Harrison (1832–1892), first lady of Benjamin Harrison, was also a schoolteacher.

In 1865, after two successful careers, first as a pianist and then a composer, Franz Liszt nearly entered the priesthood, but instead became a teacher of piano and composition.

Because the Civil War had closed his school in Georgia, Woodrow Wilson was homeschooled until he was nine. Wilson suffered from a type of dyslexia that slowed his learning to read. He did eventually make up for lost time, however, and became a schoolteacher, writer of textbooks, and a college president before running for public office.

First ladies who were once teachers include Grace Goodhue Coolidge. She was talkative and fun loving, the opposite of her husband, Calvin. In 1904, when Calvin Coolidge met her, she was a teacher at the Clarke School for the Deaf in Northampton, Massachusetts.

Maxfield Parrish and N. C. Wyeth both had the same art teacher: illustrator, artist, and children's book author Howard Pyle (1853–1911).

A literature teacher wrote the words to "America, the Beautiful." Katharine Lee Bates (1859–1929) composed the words in 1893 after she was inspired by a spectacular view from atop Pikes Peak in Colorado. Somebody set the poem to the melody "Materna" (1882) by American composer Samuel Augustus Ward, and a song was born. Bates later became a full professor at Wellesley College, one of the few women at the time to hold that rank.

Before he invented the telephone, Alexander Graham Bell opened a school for teachers of the deaf in Boston. He later became a professor at Boston University.

One of the most famous instructors of the twentieth century was Anne Sullivan (1866–1936), teacher of Helen Keller, the deaf and blind woman who won international fame as a writer and lecturer. What most people don't know is how well suited Sullivan was for the job. She herself was nearly without sight as a child. Sent to the Perkins Institution for the Blind in Boston for schooling, she roomed with Laura Bridgman, the first deaf and blind person educated in the United States. Sullivan eventually underwent surgery that restored most of her vision, and she became a teacher.

Before attending university, Marie Curie (1867–1934) began an illegal, clandestine school in Poland to teach the children of factory workers. As Poland was under Russian rule at the time, there would have been horrible consequences if young Marie had been caught.

The descendents of two educators from Louisville, Kentucky, got very rich because they wrote the song that became "Happy Birthday to You." In 1894, teacher Mildred Hill and her sister and principal Dr. Patty Hill wrote a song called "Good Morning to All." A music publisher, apparently thinking the song was in the public domain, changed a few words and printed it in a songbook as "Happy Birthday to You." After the lawsuits settled, the two teachers ended up owning copyrights to both songs. It's believed to be the most-performed song ever, and the Hills' estates continue to collect royalties on it and will until 2010.

A teacher originated Mother's Day. Anna Jarvis of West Virginia was filled with regret and guilt after her mother died in 1902. During the next decade she worked tirelessly to get motherhood recognized by cities, towns, and states across the nation. Finally in 1914, seeing a mom-and-apple-pie no-brainer political decision, the United States Congress made Mother's Day a national holiday. It became particularly popular among florists (10 million bouquets of flowers), greeting card makers (150 million greeting cards), and especially long-distance carriers and restaurateurs. (Mother's Day is the biggest day of the year for long-distance calls and eat-out meals.)

What became of Miss Jarvis? She had quit her teaching job for the campaign. She became quite upset by the commercialization of what she had visualized as a religious holiday; each Mother's Day began to feel like a painful mockery of her life and ideals. Add to that the heartbreak of a painful love affair, Jarvis remained unmarried and childless. She died alone in 1948, a poverty-stricken recluse, at the age of eighty-eight.

In 1903, a Russian high school teacher named Konstantin E. Tsiolkovsky wrote the first scientific paper on the idea of using of rockets for space travel.

Surfing teacher George Freeth introduced the sport of surfing to the American mainland, thanks to the generosity of writer Jack London. After learning to surf with Freeth in Hawaii in 1907, London was ecstatic about it. It's said that if London hadn't brought Freeth to California to teach and do surfing exhibitions, the sport very well may have disappeared into obscurity.

Nikolai Rimsky-Korsakov was not only an accomplished composer but an accomplished music teacher as well, at the St. Petersburg Conservatory. Several of his students became important composers, including Sergei Prokofiev and Igor Stravinsky. In 1913, he wrote a textbook, *Principles of Orchestration,* that is still used today.

When Einstein originally graduated from university, there were no teaching jobs available for him, so he went to work in a patent office. This turned out to be ideal, giving him time to focus on physics. He wrote five brilliant papers on various theories, which earned him a doctorate and won him the teaching job he'd been yearning for. Oh yeah, and the papers also completely changed the way the world understood physics.

Although Einstein was glad to be an academic, though he never saw it as anything more than a hobby, considering himself somewhat of a failure in life. What he really wanted to do with his life was play the concert violin, alas.

Does the name "Gail Borden" ring a bell? Well, maybe not, but he was the inventor of condensed milk and founder of the milk product company that bears his name. Before that, he was the founder of Texas' largest newspaper and originated the rallying cry, "Remember the Alamo!" Before that, though, he was a schoolteacher.

Virginia Woolf was briefly a teacher. It didn't last long. She said later that the experience was too unnerving: "I can tell you the first sentence of my lecture: 'The poet Keats died when he was twenty-five; and he wrote all of his work before that.'"

It was a science teacher who invented the fill-in-the-circle test form. His name was Reynold Johnson, and his teaching career spanned the Great Depression. But the optical scan form wasn't his biggest claim to fame. For IBM, he also invented the RAMAC 305, the first hard disk drive, which held five megabytes of data on plates that weighed in at five tons.

Any schoolkid will tell you that this makes perfect sense: Before Benito Mussolini became the dictator *Il Duce* of Italy, he was a schoolteacher.

Golda Meir, when just a girl, wanted nothing more than to be a schoolteacher. She begged her parents to let her attend a teachers' college, but they refused. Pre-1920s, girls simply didn't go to college. Eventually, she ran away from home and adopted Zionism, her parents relented, and Meir attended Milwaukee Teachers Training College. By the time she was through with her education, however, her dreams were laid aside as politics called. She never realized her wish to be a teacher, and had to settle for prime minister of a new country, instead.

It wasn't those creative Japanese who invented the Tonka toy truck, but a group of resourceful schoolteachers from Minnesota. In 1957, after buying materials to make garden tools to supplement their incomes, a group of teachers decided the task of marketing and selling was too much trouble. They used the leftover materials to make children's toys for personal use. A truck didn't look too bad, so on a whim they shopped it around to toy stores. It was a hit.

The name for the trucks comes from the lake near their community—Lake Minnetonka. The teachers, ever-punning group of professionals that they are, called the trucks "mini-Tonka trucks." More than 30 million toy trucks later, the rest is toy history.

Robert Lawrence Stine tried his hand at teaching junior high school for a year, but decided he couldn't hack it. After a long stint at Scholastic Books, he decided that he'd be better at writing for junior high kids than teaching them. He was right—his Goosebumps series has sold millions of copies.

Which former teacher turned screen star would you have preferred to study under? Here are some choices: Will ("Grandpa Walton") Geer, Margaret ("Wicked Witch of the West") Hamilton, or Madeleine ("Blazing Saddles") Kahn?

Heartthrob actor Ben Affleck's mom is a teacher.

Folk singer/songwriter/actor Kris Kristofferson was once a teacher at West Point. He had been a Rhodes Scholar as well.

You know singer/songwriter Sting? He also once made his living as a teacher.

Before becoming a rock star, Mick Jagger was a student at the prestigious London School of Economics.

Another rock 'n' roller, Gene Simmons of the '70s group Kiss, was a high school teacher. He taught at a public school in Spanish Harlem while moonlighting on his music career. His tenure at Public School 75 was somewhat tenuous. He broke ranks with traditional English curriculum by using *Spiderman* comic books as teaching aids instead of classic Western literature.

Years before, Simmons had written a college English term paper on "The Social Significance of the Panel Graphic Art Form" devoted to the impact of comic strips on American culture.

Simmons' teaching didn't last long, but it wasn't because of the comic books. He left on his own accord to devote more time to his music.

Singer Sheryl Crow, while waiting for her big break into music, taught elementary school music to autistic children in the St. Louis, Missouri, public school system.

SIX

Before They Were Famous

Where did William Shakespeare learn his command of the English language? All evidence indicates that the Bard never went beyond elementary school, namely the King's New School, the local grammar school in Stratford-on-Avon. While the main course of study there was Latin, students like young Willie were also taught logic, ethics, rhetoric, and the classical literature of Plutarch, Horace, Cicero, Virgil, and Ovid.

Report Card: Here are some of the more devastating remarks made by teachers to some noted names:

"Dull and inept . . . " —in reference to young James Watt

"Addled, backward dunce." —in reference to young Thomas Edison

"Your brain is a lump of white fat." —in reference to young G. K. Chesterson

"The stupidest boy at Harrow School." —in reference to young Winston Churchill

"You will be a disgrace to yourself and all your family." —in reference to young Charles Darwin

"You will never amount to anything, Einstein!" —in reference to young Albert Einstein

Tony Bennett's teacher divided her classroom into two groups: "Golden Birds," those who could sing, and "Blackbirds," those who could not. Incredibly, Tony was placed in the Blackbirds group.

Elvis Presley tried out for the glee club in high school but was rejected because his singing voice wasn't good enough. Ouch!

Because of his father's death, Samuel "Mark Twain" Clemens left school at twelve.

"I have never let my schooling interfere with my education."

—*Mark Twain*

Young Tom Edison

At the age of eight, Thomas Edison was enrolled in a one-room school run by one Rev. Alva Engle, a tough teacher who wielded a leather strap as a teaching aid. After three months of insults and beatings, Engle told Edison that his mind was "backward." It was more than the boy could take and he ran out of the schoolroom.

Modern experts believe Edison had dyslexia, complicated by near-deafness. He didn't learn to talk until he was four. Reading, writing, and especially spelling bedeviled him for the rest of his life.

Edison never did return to school. His mother taught him at home from then on.

Years later, Rev. Engle had the gall to write to the then successful electrical tycoon to remind him that the school had forgiven his unpaid tuition years earlier. But he was retired now "and as you now have a large income, I thought perhaps you would be glad to render me a little aid." Edison thought the matter over, and then sent him a check for $25.

Cutting Class

"Don't drop out of high school, you'll never make anything of yourself." Tell that to Henry Ford, Mary Baker Eddy, Orville and Wilbur Wright, George Gershwin, Frank Sinatra, Dean Martin, D. W. Griffith, Jack London, Al Pacino, Rod McKuen, Harry Belafonte, and Cher.

The winner of the first Nobel Peace Prize in 1901, Jean Henri Dunant, was a grade school drop-out.

How many presidents were grammar school drop-outs? Three: Andrew Jackson, Andrew Johnson, and Zachary Taylor.

Another grammar school drop-out was industrialist Andrew Carnegie. Not that he didn't value education. He gave the lion's share of his fortune to found educational institutions, including more than 2,500 public libraries throughout the world, a group of technical schools that became Carnegie Mellon University, the Carnegie Institution of Washington to encourage research in the biological and physical sciences, and Carnegie Hall.

Other elementary school drop-outs include labor leader Samuel Gompers, politician Al Smith, march king John Phillips Sousa, writer Charles Dickens, actor Charlie Chaplin, artist Claude Monet, dancer Isadora Duncan, showman Buffalo Bill Cody, and songwriter Noel Coward.

Richard Jenkins was an orphaned son of a Welsh coal miner. His English teacher, Philip Burton, encouraged young him to become an actor and even took young Richie on as his ward. The boy decided to adopt his teacher's last name and wisely took his advice. Instead of becoming a coal miner, Richie Jenkins did pretty well for himself as actor Richard Burton.

Two of America's early influential writers—poet Henry Wadsworth Longfellow and novelist Nathaniel Hawthorne—were classmates at Bowdoin College in Brunswick, Maine.

Two unlikely classmates: Putter Arnold Palmer and puppeteer Fred Rogers were high school buddies in Youngstown, Pennsylvania.

Novelist Edgar Allen Poe, painter James Whistler, and mind traveler Timothy Leary were all once students at West Point Military Academy. Not surprisingly, none of them made it through to graduation nor to an officership in the military.

Poe flunked out in a particularly spectacular way. An order came for cadets to show up for a full-dress parade wearing "white belt and gloves, under arms." He followed the order all too literally, appearing wearing nothing but a belt, and carrying his gloves under his naked arms.

Where did Ben meet Jerry? The ice cream magnates met while trailing behind their classmates running laps in high school gym class. "We were nerds," said Jerry Greenfield about the beginning of his friendship with Ben Cohen, "the two slowest, fattest guys in class."

Salvador Dali was expelled from art school in 1926 for refusing to allow teachers to critique his paintings.

Former sportscaster Howard Cosell was a super-smart Phi Beta Kappa. So was African American singer and civil rights advocate Paul Robeson, 1920s tennis champion Helen Newington Wills, and politician Edmund Muskie.

Who says being a school cheerleader isn't a springboard to fame and fortune? Former cheerleaders include Calista Flockhart, Lily Tomlin, Raquel Welch, Dinah Shore,

Patty Hearst, Carly Simon, Ann-Margret, Cybill Shepherd, Trent Lott, Dwight Eisenhower, and Gerald Ford.

On the other hand, so was Lynette "Squeaky" Fromme, who tried to assassinate former fellow cheerleader Ford.

Louis Armstrong, who grew up in New Orleans' toughest neighborhood, was sent at thirteen to finish his education at the Colored Waif's Home after he fired a gun at someone. Luckily, the school had a band program, and young Louis learned to play the trumpet there.

Ted Geisel got kicked off the college humor magazine as a punishment for having a still in his dorm room at Dartmouth during Prohibition. He simply started using his middle name "Seuss" and kept writing. Later, when he decided to write kids' books, he added "Dr." in front of it to sound more legitimate.

Years later in 1957, Dartmouth gave Geisel an honorary doctorate. And that's the story of how "Dr. Seuss" became a real doctor.

Here's something to think about the next time you eat a Hershey's bar. Milton Hershey didn't particularly care about getting rich. He decided to start the Milton Hershey School for Orphaned Boys with a good chunk of his profits. The school trust still owns 56 percent of the Hershey Company stock.

During the days at Cambridge when Lord Byron attended, there was a firm rule that no dogs were allowed to be kept in the students' rooms. Byron had no problem with this rule. He got a pet bear.

In high school Marilyn Monroe was a journalist on the school paper. One of her articles mentioned that "53% of the gentlemen prefer blondes as their dream girl."

When Marilyn Monroe was a little girl, all she really wanted was to be a teacher and "own a lot of dogs."

The '70s southern rock band Lynyrd Skynyrd got their name from a hated high school gym teacher in Jacksonville, Florida—a man named Leonard Skinner.

Mr. Skinner was tough when the boys were in school. Skinner once admitted, "I was in my younger days pretty intense, I guess."

Despite their early relationship Skinner and band members stayed in touch over the years, Skinner even attending the funeral of band member Leon Wilkeson—his favorite from the old gang of young misfits.

Before the British comedy team came up with the name Monty Python's Flying Circus, there were other ideas bandied about. There was "A Horse, a Spoon and a Basic," "Bunn, Wackett, Buzzard, Stubble and Boot," "The Toad Elevating

Moment," and "Gwen Dibley's Flying Circus." The last one was inspired by Michael Palin's childhood piano teacher—Ms. Gwen Dibley.

"Education is what remains after one has forgotten everything he learned in school."

—Albert Einstein

Harpo, of Marx Brothers fame, was in the second grade when he decided he'd had enough. Enough of being dropped, that is. Some class rapscallions kept tossing him out of a window whenever the teacher left the room. Harpo dropped out of school.

Chico Marx was a whiz at math. Instead of continuing on with his education, however, he dropped out of school at twelve to use his math skills to hustle a little pool.

Because he didn't grasp many other subjects except math and literature, Albert Einstein's teachers dubbed him "Herr Langweil," meaning "Mr. Dullard." No matter the amount of abuse, Einstein said he simply wasn't willing to "pretend to learn." Despite these setbacks, Einstein did eventually finish and go on to college.

Abbie Hoffman, founder of the Yippies (the radical Youth International Party of the '60s) wrote his sophomore paper on atheism, defending its principles. Upon learning of its topic, his teacher grabbed him by the collar and called him "a little Communist bastard." Abbie jumped up, overturned his teacher's desk and beat the daylights out of him. He was expelled.

While he was at Harvard, William Randolph Hearst was known to have kept a pet alligator named Champagne Charlie. The beast would often wander around campus drunk.

Not because of the alligator but because he was failing most of his subjects, Hearst was expelled from Harvard in 1885.

Richard Nixon's father loaned him money to go to law school at Duke, expecting that he pay back every cent when through. While attending, Nixon lived in a very small shack off campus. He didn't date, and once snuck into the dean's office to see his grades. His nickname during this time was "Gloomy Gus."

"What are schools for if not indoctrination against Communism?"

—*Richard Nixon*

Alfred Hitchcock didn't have fond memories of his boyhood schooling. For starters, he attended a Jesuit school where the priests exacted punishment using hard rubber canes. Second, the kids called him "Cocky." He hated it. He also hated his parents' nickname for him: "Fred." He called himself "Hitch."

General George S. Patton was dyslexic. His father kept him home from school so he wouldn't get picked on. When Patton was ready for university studies, he applied and was accepted to West Point, where he proceeded to flunk out of his freshman year. He repeated and finally passed.

When Adolf Hitler was a young chap he went to a Benedictine school. His dream at the time was to become an abbot. Eventually, he became disillusioned with religious life and began focusing on art. He tried to avoid his obligatory army stint by applying to an art school. When he failed to get accepted, he went ahead and enlisted.

Malcolm Forbes and George Shultz went to school together. When Forbes received a duplicating machine for his thirteenth birthday, the two put their heads and pens together and created a school newspaper.

One of Winston Churchill's boarding school teachers characterized his time as "one long feud with authority," as he was "the naughtiest boy in the world."

Churchill was placed in a learning group with boys who were considered stupid. His schoolmaster would often pop into the class and say, "Look at the stupidest boy at Harrow who is the son of the cleverest man in England."

Art Garfunkel and Paul Simon attended Public School 164 together in Queens, New York. By the ages of fourteen, they were writing songs. At fifteen they signed their first record contract and recorded their first hit, aptly named "Hey Schoolgirl."

seven

Tools of the Trade

"A child's life is like a piece of paper on which every passerby leaves a mark."

—*Old Chinese proverb*

The Pen Is Mightier Than the Sword

Before the modern pen, students used quills made from feathers that had to be dipped into ink every few words. The tips of the feathers had to be re-cut and sharpened frequently.

If you like that retro quill pen look, take a wing feather from a large bird and harden it by heating it or leaving it in the sun for a month or two. Cut the end on a diagonal, putting a slit down the middle of the point. This creates a flexible point that, depending on the amount of pressure you use, produces thin to thick strokes.

The quill pen was state-of-the-art for writing tools for about 1,300 years, from 500 to 1803 C.E., when English engineer Bryan Donkin patented a steel pen point. It still needed to be dipped into ink every few words. Enter Lewis Waterman, a New York insurance agent who was tired of continually dipping for ink. In 1884, he patented the first practical fountain pen.

John J. Loud was first to patent a ballpoint pen-type contraption in 1888. His was called the "rolling-pointed fountain marker." In fact, over the next thirty years, 350 similar patents were issued by the United States Patent Office. But none of them proved dependably workable.

It was not that long ago—1938—that George and Lazlo Biro from Hungary patented the first *workable* ballpoint pen. It was very similar to that cheap Bic pen you hold in your hand.

With the worldwide depression and war, marketing was slow. However, bomber crews loved the new pens because they didn't leak at high altitudes like fountain pens would when the air pressure inside the pen became greater than the air pressure outside it.

After the war, the new ballpoint pen was a novelty. When it was introduced at Gimbel's department store in 1945, they quickly sold out for $12.50 each (about $118.25 in today's money). Unfortunately, there were still a few bugs in the ink design, and the pens tended to clog in cold weather . . . and ooze ink in hot.

Finally, a French penmaker named Marcel Bich entered the picture. Bich had watched the ballpoint pen debacle with professional interest. Interested in the concept, but appalled at the pen's high price and low quality, he decided to try his hand at it. He licensed the Biro design, but also bought every brand of ballpoint imitators, looking for their strengths and weaknesses. Finally, in 1952, he unveiled his triumph: an inexpensive transparent, six-sided plastic pen that wrote smoothly and dependably.

That classic is still with us. The only mystery is this—why is it called the Bic pen instead of the Bich pen? Well, that's easy. Looking at the international market, Bich realized that he'd have a problem with the spelling of his name. He changed the spelling of his name so that it would be pronounced correctly wherever the pen was sold—"Bic."

Waxing Artistic

It was a schoolteacher who coined the brand name "Crayola." Alice Binney's husband Edwin was the Binney in Binney & Smith, the popular crayon's manufacturer.

When in the early 1900s Binney & Smith expanded their line from paint pigments and barn paint to include schoolroom slate pencils, they heard from Alice and other teachers that two of their pet peeves (besides low pay and bad conditions) were crumbly chalk and expensive imported crayons. This feedback from teachers led to Binney and Smith creating "dustless chalk" and Crayolas.

Want to know what that distinctive crayon smell is? Maybe you don't. It's stearic acid, also known as beef fat.

The first two crayons in a box to be worn down to nubs are usually the black followed by the red.

Get a Lead Up

Pencils are the writing instrument of choice of astronauts, because unlike most pens, they write dependably in zero-gravity.

Why is a pencil "lead" called that—did pencils ever have lead in them? They've always had a mixture of lead and graphite. But there was a time when graphite was thought to be a type of lead, and so the name stuck.

Graphite, a carbon compound, has been used for writing since before pencils were invented. In 1789 geologist Abraham Werner named the mineral from a Greek word meaning "to write."

Take out your No. 2 pencil. . . . What makes a pencil lead darker and softer like a No. 3 pencil, or lighter and harder like a No. 1? It depends on the mixture of clay and graphite. The more graphite, the darker and softer the lead is. This is something early manufacturers figured out in 1795, back when graphite was used as an uncovered chalk crayon—powdered graphite was mixed with clay and baked into flat writing strips.

Sometimes people, tired of getting their hands blackened, would wrap the graphite tightly in a string that they could unwrap as the graphite got shorter. Finally, in 1812 American William Monroe invented the process still used today of encasing a tiny piece of graphite inside an outer case of incense cedar.

Mechanical pencils weren't invented until 1877. The basic design changed little for 99 years until in 1976, when mechanical pencils made a quantum leap forward—somebody figured out a way to store a dozen leads inside the pencil, allowing it to automatically feed one lead after another instead of constantly adding a new stick of lead.

Here's how pencils are made, thanks to William Monroe. Take a board of soft wood and cut a series of lead-sized grooves in it. After you've shaped the graphite-clay leads from an extruder and hardened them at 120° F., lay them into each groove. Glue a similarly grooved board upside down on top of the first board, covering the leads in a wood sandwich. Cut out each wood-enclosed lead and shape it to round or hexagonal. Paint it and attach a rubber eraser to one end. Simple!

Then how come we can never find one when we need one? The world generates more than 10 billion pencils every year. Two billion of these come from the United States. No, not all from Pencilvania.

The most popular color for painting the outside of pencils is yellow. Why? No particular reason, actually.

The metal band that holds the eraser on is called a *ferrule.*

Colored pencils are made in a similar way to black pencils, but dyes and pigments are mixed with clay instead of graphite.

Why are most pencils hexagonal—do the six sides enhance your grip? Maybe, but the main reason is that round pencils roll off tables and desks easily—hexagonal ones don't.

That little hole in the middle of your pencil sharpener that your pencil goes into has its own name. It's called a *chuck.*

Take a look at that eraser and realize that you have a little bit of history in your hand. In 1770, English chemist Joseph Priestley discovered that latex could be used to rub out pencil marks. It's from this use that we got the name "rubber."

Most other uses of rubber had to wait until Charles Goodyear discovered vulcanization. That was in 1839, and it was only six years later that London inventor Stephen Perry invented that classroom necessity, the rubber band.

The felt-tip pen may seem like it's been in classrooms forever, but it was introduced to the United States the same year that John Kennedy was assassinated and Beatlemania began (1963, of course). It had been invented a year earlier by Yukio Horie of Japan. Horie's purpose was simple: to create a pen that would be suited to the strokes of Japanese writing, traditionally done with a pointed ink brush.

Actually, "felt" tip can be a misnomer—the pen's tip is usually made of nylon or some other synthetic fiber. The ink is fed to the tip using an elaborate system of capillary action.

What's Black and White and Read All Over?

True felt is made from wool or other animal fibers that have been steamed and flattened into a cloth. It does make a regular appearance in the classroom as the business side of your chalkboard eraser.

Chemically, chalk is almost pure calcium carbonate with mere traces of other minerals.

Chalk is a natural product, a soft form of limestone made up of the remains of small marine organisms that sunk into the mud of an ancient sea. Millions of creatures gave their lives for that simple stick of chalk in your hand.

Where is chalk found naturally? Lots of places. The largest, though, are in the southwest United States, and the southern part of the British Isles. The White Cliffs of Dover are made of chalk, and by themselves could keep classrooms supplied for millions of years.

Chalk is particularly found in earth layers from the Cretaceous Period, which started about 138 million years ago and lasted for 73 million years. That's why, when scientists were wracking their brains for a good name for the era, they settled on *creta,* the Latin word for chalk.

Chalkboards are made from slate, glass, wood, or porcelain on steel. They're still commonly called "blackboards," even when green, gray, blue, brown, or red.

Pulp Facts and Fiction

What would a classroom be without paper? Actually, until the 1800s paper was expensive and scarce, and students primarily did their schoolwork on slates and read their lessons from hornbooks. The slate—a thin piece of rock that could be written on with chalk or charcoal crayons—was erasable and was used over and over again.

Hornbooks were flat boards with a handle. The teacher attached precious scraps of paper with lessons on them. The lesson board and paper were covered with a thin piece of animal horn, flattened and made transparent by boiling and scraping, that protected the paper from the ravages of weather, wear, and students.

Be glad you have paper. Romans in the first century C.E. had papyrus, but students almost never used it. Instead, they scratched their writing exercises with pointed metal or bone into wax that coated a wooden tablet. After the lesson was done, they could smooth out the wax and start again with a clean slate, as it were.

The word *paper* comes from "papyrus," which was much more difficult to make than paper and expensive. The ancient Egyptians made it by layering strips of the papyrus plant's stem. When placed under pressure, the crushed strips matted into a porous, white paper.

Papyrus was gradually replaced by parchment, which was more expensive but more durable (in fact, examples have survived from 1500 B.C.E.). Parchment was made from the skins of sheep, goats, or calves that were placed in lime to remove the hair and fat, stretched, scraped, and then rubbed with chalk and pumice to create a smooth, white writing surface.

It was the ancient Chinese who discovered how to make paper. They first used the fiber from hemp and the inner bark from the mulberry trees that were a byproduct of the silk trade. (Silkworms live exclusively on mulberry leaves.) Later they figured out that a good paper could be made from rags, rope, and old fishing nets that were pounded into a pulp.

In the New World, in about 500 C.E., the Mayans made a similar discovery, using bark from fig leaves that was beaten and treated with lime to make writing materials. Later, the Aztecs improved the method further.

Like most Chinese inventions, paper-making was kept secret from the rest of the world. Finally, in the eighth century, several

Chinese papermakers were captured by Arabs in what is now western Turkestan, and the paper tiger was out of the bag. Baghdad developed a flourishing paper industry in 795 C.E., and the Crusades and Moor invasions spread the art to Europe.

The first American paper mill opened in Philadelphia in 1690.

There was a problem worldwide through the sixteenth and seventeenth centuries—an extreme paper shortage. Humanity had long forgotten what the early Chinese and Mayans knew—that paper could be made from hemp and wood pulp. With the printing press, new empires, and the rise of a business class, demand of paper hit a fever pitch, but the supply of old rags could not keep up.

One papermaker got so desperate that he bought a huge quantity of the cloth wrappings from ancient Egyptian mummies. Unfortunately, many of his customers got seriously ill, so he abandoned that strategy.

Eventually, it was a wasp nest in the woods that led modern humanity back to wood pulp for making paper. René-Antoine Ferchault de Éaumer, perhaps France's greatest scientist, went for a restful walk in the woods and found an abandoned paper wasp nest. He realized that the wasps were able to make fine paper with nothing but wood pulp and their digestive juices. If they can do it, he wrote in a paper in 1719, why can't we?

Although Éaumer set off a flurry of experimentation with his paper, it took more than a century before people figured out how to make a quality wood-pulp paper using mechanical grinders and sulfurous acid to break down the fibers. By the 1880s, most paper was made of wood pulp.

Those long rolls of brown art paper that we call Kraft paper? It's not the name of the maker or because we use them for crafts—*kraft* means "strong" in German.

The Inside Story on Books

The McGuffey Readers were probably the most influential pieces of literature in American schools. Written by Rev. William Holmes McGuffey in 1833, these first-course textbooks taught the basics of history, biology, arithmetic, literature, argumentation, philosophy, and religion, peppered with ideals of good manners, honesty, and kindness.

Before the McGuffey Reader, there was the *New England Primer,* first printed in Boston in 1690 and used for more than a century by schoolkids. Over 5 million were sold. Puritans believed that illiteracy was a plot by Satan to keep people from the Scriptures. (In fact, a 1642 law made it illegal for any child in Massachusetts to not learn to read.)

The *Primer* used every opportunity to teach a grim sort of religion. For example, this alphabet lesson:

A in Adam's Fall
We sinned all.
B They Life to Mend
This book Attend.
C The Cat doth play
And after slay.
D A dog will bite
A Thief at night.
E An Eagle's flight
Is Out of sight.
F The Idle Fool
Is Whipt at School. . . .

The *New England Primer*, by the way, is also the source of the children's prayer that begins, "Now I lay me down to sleep. . . ."

Before Noah Webster wrote his dictionary of renown, he first wrote the now-famous "blue-backed" spelling book. Just like his dictionary, it was a bestseller, too, selling more than 100 million copies. His early grammar book was also wildly popular among the young set.

Noah Webster is responsible for changing the way we spell several words. The original spelling of *music* was "musick," but Webster thought it redundant. He changed "plough" to "plow," and "centre" to "center." He also changed the pronunciation of "tion" from "she-un" to "shun."

Webster spent over twenty years researching in England, France, and the United States to find the origins of many of the words that appear in the Webster's dictionary. His original edition contained 70,000 English words, with their official spelling, origin, pronunciation, and definition.

The world's most ambitious encyclopedia ever was the *Yung-Lo ta-tien* from China's Ming dynasty (1368–1644). About 2,000 scholars labored for five years to produce 11,000 volumes that detailed much of what was known up to that point. It was too costly to print, so only two copies were made by hand.

Xeroxing worksheets for the class? The Xerox method of copying—using light, an electric charge, and dry powder—is called "xerography" and was developed and patented by physicist Chester F. Carlson. *Xerography* is from the Greek, meaning "dry writing." The Haloid Company of Rochester, New York, bought the patent, changed their name to Xerox, and made an empire off of Carlson's process.

The Rubik's Cube was designed as a teaching aid for Hungarian math students. Mathematician Erno Rubik thought it up in 1974 and realized not long after that it had commercial appeal.

Not-so-coincidentally, math teacher Erno Rubik became the first person in a Communist country to make a million dollars.

"You can't wipe away tears with notebook paper."

—*Charles Schultz*

The first paper clip was invented in 1899 by a Norwegian patent clerk named Johann Vaaler. A monument to him, shaped like a giant paperclip, stands near Oslo.

Norwegians take pride in Vaaler and his wiry invention. During the Nazi occupation, Norwegians wore paperclips in their lapels as a sign of nationalism and resistance.

eight

Teacher Appreciation

"One must have as much respect for the teacher as for God."

—The Talmud

National Teacher Day comes on a different day each year. Why? Because the first full week of May is Teacher Appreciation Week, and the Tuesday during that week is actually National Teacher Day. Man, a week *and* a day. Lucky dogs.

Maulana. That's Swahili for "master teacher." Impress your friends.

Minerva was not only the ancient Roman goddess of education, but also of those closely related realms, like craftsmen and war.

Salary blues? Consider the slogan for the aptly named Teacher's Scotch Whiskey: "Rich is better." There are some school board members who could stand to take it to heart. Send them a bottle.

And finally consider this as you head back into the classroom: According to some research, the more education a woman has, the less likely she is to find someone to be happily partnered with. Probably because the more and more knowledge she gains, the smaller the pool of eligible educated equals she has to choose from. We imagine this works the opposite way, too: The more educated the man, the less likely he is to find a partner to settle down with.

Helpful Hints

"The teacher who is indeed wise does not bid you to enter the house of his wisdom but rather leads you to the threshold of your mind."

—Kahlil Gibran

"For every person wishing to teach there are thirty not wanting to be taught."

—W. C. Sellar and R. J. Yeatman

"Teaching is not a lost art, but the regard for it is a lost tradition."

—Jacques Barzun

"It would be a great advantage to some teachers if they would steal two hours a day from their pupils, and give their own minds the benefit of the robbery."

—*J. F. Boyse*

"Thoroughly to teach another is the best way to learn for yourself."

—*Tryon Edwards*

"Those who can, teach. Those who can't, go into some less significant line of work."

—*Unknown*

"Good teaching is ¼ preparation and ¾ theater."

—*Gail Godwin*

"The object of teaching a child is to enable him to get along without a teacher."

—*Elbert Hubbard*

"Teachers are people who start things they never see finished, and for which they never get thanks until it is too late."

—Max Forman

"He that teaches himself hath a fool for his master."

—Benjamin Franklin

"You cannot teach a man anything; you can only help him find it within himself."

—Galileo Galilei

"Teachers who educate children deserve more honor than parents, who merely gave them birth. For the latter provided mere life, while the former ensured a good life."

—Aristotle

"**O**ne teacher is better than two books."

—Old German proverb

"**O**ne good teacher in a lifetime may sometimes change a delinquent into a solid citizen."

—Philip Wylie

"**T**he teacher cannot build positive self-concepts in students without building his own."

—William Purkey

"**I** am indebted to my father for living, but to my teacher for living well."

—Alexander the Great, referring to Aristotle

"Those that do teach young babes,
Do it with gentle means and easy tasks."

—*Shakespeare's* Othello

"The more you prepare outside class, the less you perspire in class. The less you perspire in class, the more you inspire the class."

—*Ho Boon Tiong*

"A teacher who is attempting to teach, without inspiring the pupil with a desire to learn, is hammering on a cold iron."

—*Horace Mann*

"The task of the modern educator is not to cut down jungles, but to irrigate ditches."

—*C. S. Lewis*

"**A** teacher affects eternity; he can never tell where his influence stops."

—Henry Adams, from The Education of Henry Adams

"**N**ot many of you should presume to be a teacher, my brethren, because you know that we who teach will be judged more strictly."

—James 3:1

"**I**f your plan is for one year, plant rice; If your plan is for ten years, plant trees; If your plan is for 100 years, educate children."

—Confucius

"**W**hen the pupil is ready, the teacher will come."

—Old Chinese proverb

"To know how to suggest is the art of teaching."

—Henri Frederic Amiel, nineteenth-century Swiss humorist and critic

"I cannot teach you; only help you to explore yourself."

—Bruce Lee

"If history were taught in the form of stories, it would never be forgotten."

—Rudyard Kipling

"You cannot but think that to apperceive your pupil as a little sensitive, impulsive, associative, and reactive organism, partly fated and partly free, will lead to a better intelligence of all his ways. Understand him, then as such a subtle little piece of machinery. And if, in addition, you can also see him *sub specie boni,* and love him as well, you will be in the best possible position for becoming perfect teachers."

—*William James*

"To think is to differ."

—*Clarence Darrow*

Saints Preserve Us

Maybe this is worth getting a statuette for your workspace: Among Roman Catholics, Saint John De La Salle is the patron saint of teachers.

Saint Thomas Aquinas is the patron saint of schools and scholars.

Saint Genesius is the patron saint of dancing teachers.

Saint Hubert is the patron saint of math teachers.

Saint Cecille and Saint Gregory are patron saints of choral and band teachers.

Saint Luke is the patron saint of art teachers.

Saint Christopher is the patron saint of school bus drivers.

Saint Anthony is the patron saint of the school lost and found bin.

Saint Catherine is the patron saint of librarians and school secretaries.

Saint Penafort is the patron saint of law schools.

The patron saint of youth is Saint John Berchman. Of children, Saint Nicholas. And of "unruly children," Saint Sebastian.

Credited by the Vatican for writing the first European encyclopedia in the sixth century, Saint Isadore of Seville is the patron saint of schoolchildren, computer programmers, and the Internet.

But if none of these do it for you, both Saint Rita and Saint Jude are patron saints for "desperate people."

nine

Fightin' Words

"Public schools are the nurseries of all vice and immorality."

—Henry Fielding

"We are shut up in schools and college recitation rooms for ten or fifteen years, and come out at last with a bellyful of words and do not know a thing."

—Ralph Waldo Emerson

"It is little short of a miracle that modern methods of instruction have not already completely strangled the holy curiosity of inquiry. . . . I believe that if one could even deprive a healthy beast of prey of its voraciousness if on could force it with a whip to eat continuously whether it were hungry or not. . . ."

—Albert Einstein

"The schools ain't what they used to be and never was."

—*Will Rogers*

"There is that indescribable freshness and unconsciousness about an illiterate person that humbles and mocks the power of the noblest expressive genius."

—*Walt Whitman*

"Intelligence appears to be the thing that enables a man to get along without education. Education appears to be the thing that enables a man to get along without the use of his intelligence."

—*A. E. Wiggan*

"One of the ultimate advantages of an education is simply coming to the end of it."

—*B. F. Skinner*

"We're drowning in information and starving for knowledge."

—Rutherford Rogers

"Creative minds have always been known to survive any kind of bad training."

—Anna Freud

"Nothing that is worth knowing can be taught."

—Oscar Wilde

"If you keep your mind sufficiently opened, people will throw a lot of rubbish into it."

—William Orton

"Aristotle taught that the brain exists merely to cool the blood and is not involved in the process of thinking. This is true only of certain persons."

—Will Cuppy

Something to consider before loading your students with mind-numbing busywork: "As lamps are extinguished from too much oil, so it the mind from too much studying." So said French writer Michel de Montaigne in 1580.

"He who can does. He who can't, teaches."

—George Bernard Shaw

"He who can does. He who can't, teaches. He who can't teach, teaches P.E."

—Anonymous

ten

Teaching by the Numbers

In 1900, only 10 percent of American adolescents age 14–17 were enrolled in high schools.

By the end of the century the number of high school graduates increased from about 6 percent to 85 percent of all adolescents.

In 1900, about 2 percent of Americans age 18–24 were enrolled in a college. By the end of the century, more than 60 percent were.

14,462: Last time we checked, that's the number of school districts in the United States.

20,282: The number of secondary schools in the United States.

24 percent: The percentage of Americans and Dutch who complete college—the highest rate in the world.

75.9 percent of all teachers are married.

12.4 percent of all teachers are single.

11.7 percent of all teachers are widowed, divorced, or separated.

2.9 million teachers provide instruction in public elementary and secondary schools. That includes 1,620,000 elementary school teachers (including pre-kindergarten and kindergarten teachers), 1,031,000 secondary school teachers, and 255,000 teaching ungraded or unspecified classes.

16.1 to 1 is the ratio of all students to all teachers in the United States.

Getting our money's worth? Adjusted for inflation, the average school spending in 1940 was $961 per pupil. Fifty years later, it had grown to $5,526 per pupil.

12.3 students per teacher in Vermont and 12.5 in Massachusetts are the lowest average student/teacher ratios in the country.

22.0 to 1 in Utah and 21.0 to 1 in California are the highest student/teacher ratios.

54 percent: That's the proportion of high school students who graduate in Louisiana—the state with the worst dropout rate.

46.9 million students are enrolled in public elementary and secondary schools in the United States. 26.0 million are in pre-kindergarten through grade 6. 20.2 million are in grades 7 through 12. The remaining 0.7 million are ungraded.

About 15 percent of all American elementary or secondary students go to private schools.

850,000 students are being home-schooled.

15 percent: The amount by which home schooling has been growing every year for the past several years.

In the world, about 20 percent of all people are directly involved in the schools as students, teachers, or professors. That's not even including administrators, support personnel, or textbook providers.

In advanced countries like the United States, Canada, and Japan, make that 25 percent.

18 is the earliest age that students can legally quit school in eight states.

17 is the age in nine states and in the District of Columbia.

16 is the age in thirty-eight states.

14 is the age in one state.

62 percent of all high school graduates get at least some advanced schooling.

3,000: That's roughly the number of institutions of higher learning in the United States. Over half are privately owned, and most of these are small liberal arts colleges.

80 percent of all college students in the United States attend a state college or university.

0: The number of times the United States Constitution mentions schools or education.

70 percent is the average increase in real dollars of teachers' salaries between 1960 and 1970, in large part because of increased activism and strikes on the part of teacher unions at the time.

1 in 80: The ratio of American college students to the general population in the present day.

1 in 1,500: The ratio of American college students to the general population in 1810.

The eleventh fastest-growing occupation in America for 1996–2006, according to the Bureau of Labor Statistics "12 fastest growing occupations," is Special Education Teacher.

A dozen or so: It's a well-known fact that kids can be hazardous to your health. In their first year of school or preschool, they will get an average of 12–14 colds. Their parents will average 6 colds that year. Their teachers? Well, it depends on how long they've been teaching (and how many colds they've been previously exposed to) and how healthy they are.

Only 37 percent of all American kids are immunized against major childhood diseases by age two.

53 percent: That's the portion of preschool children who are read to daily.

88 percent of all American teenagers nationwide complete high school.

Half: The number of high school kids who report feeling safe in school.

53 percent: The number of high school students who report that other people's misbehavior interferes with their learning.

18 percent of all high school students say that they've been offered drugs in school.

13 percent of all seventeen-year-olds can be considered functionally illiterate.

52 percent of all Americans can perform "challenging tasks" in reading and arithmetic.

23 million American adults are functionally illiterate in reading, writing,and comprehension.

One-third: That's the number of American grade-schoolers who wear watches.

71 percent of the students suspended from school are boys.

10th: The average grade finished by prisoners in jail.

21 percent: The percentage of American high school students who still, despite living in the age of cynicism, want to be president.

53 percent: The proportion of high school students who say they "get most of their information from television." Twenty-seven percent of college graduates say the same thing.

50 percent: That's the proportion of U.S. shoplifters who have completed at least some college.

2,093: The calories burned each day by the average college student while sleeping, walking, standing, running, writing, dressing, studying, eating, talking, driving, and playing Ping-Pong. This has actually been studied.

50 percent: The portion of polled college students who say they nap during the day.

10 percent: The number of new piano students who will be practicing their art in five years.

71 percent: The male proportion of students who are expelled every year from U.S. public schools.

2 of 5: The portion of college students who binge drink, according to one Harvard University study.

eleven

Educational Follies

"It has been said that we have not had the three R's in America, we had the six R's; remedial readin', remedial 'ritin', and remedial 'rithmetic."

—Robert M. Hutchins

The three R's in education are Reading, Writing ('Riting), and Arithmetic ('Rithmetic), only one of which actually begins with an *R.* This coinage is usually credited to Sir William Curtis, who was Lord Mayor of London from 1752 to 1829. He wasn't trying to take liberties with the English language when he thought this up; he was somewhat illiterate and thought this was perfectly sensible. Sounds like some modern statesmen we've known. . . .

Simplified Spelling was the bright idea of Melvin Dewey, Andrew Carnegie, and Brander Matthews. The idea was to make the English language easier to learn by spelling words as they sound. *Through* became "thru," *dropped* was "dropt," and so on. In 1906, the three petitioned President Teddy Roosevelt and Congress to have about 300 words officially changed in all of the dictionaries. Roosevelt loved the idea and jumped on the bandwagon. However, other officials remained unmoved. Congress was so outraged that Roosevelt dropped the pursuit and the movement died away.

Claiming obscenity in 1930, U.S. Customs seized copies of *Candide,* Voltaire's satirical masterpiece, that were intended for literature classes at Harvard.

"Headmasters have powers at their disposal with which Prime Ministers and Presidents have never yet been invested."

—*Winston Churchill*

In 1999, Shakespeare's *Twelfth Night* was banned from schools in Merrimack, New Hampshire, after the school board passed a "prohibition of alternative lifestyle instruction" act. (The offending material had to do with a woman disguising herself as a boy to meet her beloved.)

Shakespeare's plays have often run into trouble with nervous school boards. One solution has been to try cleaning up anything that might offend the faint of heart. Thomas Bowdler's efforts in his 1818 *Family Shakespeare* gave rise to the word *bowdlerize.*

Other books that have been banned by public schools around the country include such classics as *The Color Purple* by Alice Walker, *Huckleberry Finn* by Mark Twain, *Of Mice and Men* by John Steinbeck, *I Know Why the Caged Bird Sings* by Maya Angelou, *The Bell Jar* by Sylvia Plath, *Ulysses* by James Joyce, *Silas Marner* by George Elliot, *Our Bodies, Ourselves* by the Boston Women's Health Collective, and *Little Red Riding Hood.*

During the McCarthy era, kids' cartons of schoolroom Crayolas suddenly came up missing Prussian Blue—nervous company officials were afraid that "Prussian" sounded too much like "Russian" and didn't want to be accused of being Communist sympathizers.

Well I'll Be a Monkey's Uncle

In 1925, the state of Tennessee prosecuted teacher John Scopes for the "crime" of teaching the theory of evolution in school.

How did the ACLU find Scopes, the teacher who was willing to be arrested to test an anti-evolution law in Tennessee?

They placed an ad in the newspaper seeking a teacher who was willing to test the law.

Few people remember that John Scopes actually lost his case. He was found guilty of teaching a forbidden subject and fined $100. Later, though, the conviction was reversed because of some small legal error, but the law stayed on the books.

Finally, in 1967, more than forty years after John Scopes was prosecuted, it continued to be a crime to inform Tennessee schoolchildren that a theory of evolution even existed.

Now, of course, the anti-evolution forces are at it again, masking Bible verses as "Creationist science" and pressuring school boards to teach it.

Who wouldn't want Nobel Prize-winning author, philosopher, and mathematician Bertrand Russell teaching at their school? The people of New York, apparently—after teaching for three years at UCLA, Russell was offered a job at City College in New York City in 1940, but the job was rescinded after conservative Christians objected to his liberal political views.

Teachers give heart, soul, and brains to their jobs. However Cornell University takes that a step further—it traditionally has asked its professors to donate their brains to the school for science. (Presumably after the profs are done using them.)

You think your community is apathetic toward school issues? In 1997,

Westmoreland, Kansas, had a school board election in which only one person was willing to be a candidate. Worse, nobody showed up on voting day, not even the candidate, Mike Sotelo. Since nobody won the election, the school board appointed a new member. It was not, however, Mike Sotelo.

New Jersey has a law, presumably rammed through by Irish Americans, that requires that all schoolchildren in the state must learn about the tragedies suffered by the Irish at the hands of the British during the Irish potato famine of the 1840s.

You'd Think They'd Want the Lowest-Scorers: So many Japanese soldiers volunteered to be kamikazes in the waning days of World War II that the authorities began accepting only those who scored the highest marks in their schools.

The English Teachers Association of Missouri once filed a complaint with the Federal Communications Commission against pitcher-turned-radio announcer, Dizzy Dean. Dean, known for his poor grammar—examples include things like "He was throwed out!" and "He slud into third base"—managed to retain his post and continued to corrupt the grammar of schoolchildren everywhere.

Ever wonder about the Dunce Cap? You're not alone. The Dunce Cap comes from a group of scholars who followed the teachings of the thirteenth-century philosopher and educator, John Duns Scotus, from

Duns Scotland. Although some of his ideas about education were intriguing, there were some that were downright weird. One of the latter was the belief that a conical hat would funnel knowledge into the brain. This idea fell out of favor when the humanists came along and soon the "Dunsmen" became synonymous with idiocy, as did their "Duns caps."

Get This: The Thurgood Marshall Scholarship Fund was started by the Miller Brewing Company. In 1993 the corporation gave $150,000 to the fund, but spent *twice* that much promoting it.

Early in the twentieth century, the Kansas legislature made it official state law that π could be rounded off to 3.

Later in the century, Iowa legislators tried to make it illegal to pass notes in school, but freedom of speech issues won out.

When Good Teachers Go Bad

Dale Christensen, a high school football coach in Libertyville, Illinois, once staged a fight and his own death at a pep rally to motivate the football team and fans for the game, or so was his defense. When the community became up in arms about his "motivational skit," he resigned from his job, claiming the students and athletes simply didn't understand where he was coming from.

Charles Routen won't be getting Elementary Teacher of the Year anytime soon. When he ran across a gag math quiz, he Xeroxed it and administered it to his students at Chicago's May Elementary School. Here's a sampling:

> Johnny can get $150 for a stolen Chevrolet, $250 for a stolen Jeep, and $600 for a stolen BMW. How many Jeeps will Johnny have to steal to pay for a $1,200 packet of uncut cocaine?

Mr. Routen no longer teaches at May Elementary.

Internet Myths

Many teachers have seen this and believed it to be genuine. It's been posted and e-mailed all over the Internet, reprinted by unsuspecting newspaper columnists, and even printed onto wall posters:

Rules for Teachers, 1872

1. Teachers each day will fill lamps, clean chimneys.
2. Each teacher will bring a bucket of water and a scuttle of coal for the day's session.
3. Make your pens carefully. You whittle nibs to the individual taste of the pupils.
4. Men teachers may take one evening each week for courting purposes, or two evenings a week if they go to church regularly.

5. After ten hours in school, the teachers may spend the remaining time reading the Bible or other good books.
6. Women teachers who marry or engage in unseemly conduct will be dismissed.
7. Every teacher should lay aside from each pay a goodly sum of this earnings for his benefit during his declining years so that he will not become a burden on society.
8. Any teacher who smokes, uses liquor in any form, frequents pool or public halls, or gets shaved in a barber shop will give good reason to suspect his worth, intention, integrity, and honesty.
9. The teacher who performs his labor faithfully and without fault for five years will be given an increase of twenty cents per week in his pay, providing the Board of Education approves.

Well, it's a hoax. So is a "Rules for Students," supposedly from about the same time:

1. Respect your schoolmaster. Obey him and accept his punishments.
2. Do not call your classmates names or fight with them. Love and help each other.
3. Never make noises or disturb your neighbors as they work. Be silent during classes.
4. Do not talk unless it's absolutely necessary.
5. Bring firewood into the classroom for the stove whenever the teacher tells you to.
6. If the master calls your name after class, straighten the benches and tables, sweep the room, dust, and leave everything tidy.

Both of these fake rules lists are usually accompanied by introductions talking about how much better things are today.

Aside from these two hoaxes, there is a third one—a supposed 1895 graduation exam for eighth graders in Salina, Kansas. The test appears so hard one only marvels at how dumb today's students are in comparison.

As one newspaper writer who was tricked by the "eight grade test" wrote: "The object of this exercise was only to reveal what many of us have known for some time. The dumbing down of American public education over the last 100 years has been substantial." Well, at least we now know our reporters are no smarter than in the past.

twelve

Life on Campus

"Anyone who has remained in school for up to twelve years without mounting a horse is no longer good for anything but the priesthood."

—*Einhard, ninth-century German poet*

The Chinese can probably be credited with inventing college more than 4,000 years ago.

The university with the longest history? It was the University of Constantinople, a center of classical, secular learning for more than a millennium (425–1453 C.E.).

Ashram means "forest university." The first one popped up some 3,500 years ago in India.

Medical schools in the United States used to routinely get their cadavers for dissection by graverobbing, often by the faculty and students themselves making midnight raids on local graveyards. It became the custom among grieving survivors in university towns to place iron bars on new graves and hire armed guards for two weeks until the body had time to putrefy enough to make it unusable for research.

Between 1752 and 1852, there were at least thirteen riots by citizens against grave-robbing medical schools, including one in 1788 in New York City that killed eight people and injured scores of others.

Vassar was the first all-women's college in the world. Strangely enough, it was founded by a man. A brewer named Matthew Vassar, to be exact, was interested in helping women reach higher education. In 1861 he provided the funding to get Vassar on its way.

Nineteen years later, Bryn Mawr became the first graduate school for women. It was named after its hometown of Bryn Mawr, Pennsylvania.

The Seven Sisters—a term taken from Greek mythology —is the name traditionally applied to seven women's colleges in the United States that are known for their excellent academic records. The Seven Sisters are Smith (Northampton, Massachusetts), Bryn Mawr (near Philadelphia, Pennsylvania), Radcliffe (Cambridge, Massachusetts), Barnard (New York City), Wellesley (near Boston, Massachusetts), Vassar (Poughkeepsie, New York), and Mount Holyoke (South Hadley, Massachusetts). Today, only five of these remain as women's colleges. Vassar went coed in 1969 and Radcliffe in 1999 began accepting male undergraduates as it merged with Harvard.

"**R**ead not to contradict and confute, nor to believe and take for granted; but to weigh and consider."

—Francis Bacon

Young inventors: In the 1870s, William Frisbie from Bridgeport, Connecticut, opened a bakery near Yale University. Yale students often frequented the place for pies that came in tins with his company name stamped into the bottom. Being resourceful, as students often are, they soon learned that the pans would hover and fly when tossed. To attempt to avoid passersby being hit with the flying pie tins, the students would often yell "Frisbie!" as a warning. And that was the first flying disk.

"**A** fool's brain digests philosophy into folly, science into superstition, and art into pedantry. Hence university education."

—*George Bernard Shaw*

It was Leominster, Massachusetts, in 1951 when a twenty-one-year-old art student named Don Featherstone created the first pink lawn flamingo for the Union Products company. Originally made of styrofoam, the lawn ornaments were subject to getting a little gnarled in a windstorm, or destroyed by wayward dogs. After a redesign using plastic, the pink flamingo took off and quickly became an icon of American kitsch, and Featherstone eventually became vice president of the Union Products Company.

"The primary purpose of a liberal education is to make one's mind a pleasant place in which to spend one's time."

—Sydney J. Harris

A group of conservative Harvard alumni were disgruntled that their alma mater had added science, mathematics, natural philosophy, and other newfangled innovations to the classic and religious curriculum, and so they decided to start a new college. That college was Yale University.

William James Sidis is the youngest pupil ever admitted into Harvard. By the age of eight, he could converse in eight foreign languages and he'd written four books. He tried to enroll at the university in 1907 when he was nine—about the same time he'd given a seminar there on the fourth dimension. However, Harvard delayed his application for two more years, until he was eleven.

"*Hamlet* is the tragedy of tackling a family problem too soon after college."

—*Tom Masson*

Yale, Harvard, and Princeton all used monies garnered from lotteries to get their start. Today, there are fourteen states that give all proceeds from their lotteries to education; five more states earmark a portion of the proceeds for that purpose.

"American college students are like their colleges—they have half-dulled faculties."

—*James Thurber*

The abominable college practice of goldfish swallowing began in 1939 by Lothrop Withington, Jr., on a dare. When the news of his deed spread, the Harvard University freshman was offered $10 to do it again, and he did. From there, word spread and numbskulls from other universities began to do it, making it a competition to see how many goldfish a body could stand. The Public Health Service released a report about goldfish carrying tapeworms and the trend soon fell by the wayside.

"If you feel that you have both feet planted on level ground, then the university has failed you."

—Robert Goheen, sixteenth president of Princeton University

Writer W. E. B. Dubois, Ph.D., was the first African American to receive a doctorate from Harvard.

"I find the three major administrative problems on a campus are sex for the students, athletics for the alumni, and parking for the faculty."

—Clark Kerr

Colgate University psychologists discovered through extensive research that students are able to solve math problems best when they're flat on their backs with their feet elevated. No, really.

"I was thrown out of college for cheating on the metaphysics exam; I looked into the soul of the boy next to me."

—*Woody Allen*

The trademark Nike "swoosh" was designed by a college art student, Carolyn Davidson, in the early '70s. She was paid just $35.

"A university is what a college becomes when the faculty loses interest in students."

—*J. Ciardi*

"I am not impressed with the Ivy League establishments. Of course they graduate the best—it's all they'll take, leaving to others the problem of educating the country. They will give you an education the way the banks will give you money—provided you can prove to their satisfaction that you don't need it."

—*Peter DeVries*

Owen Hendley, a cold researcher at the University of Virginia, was known to offer students $300 and four nights in a hotel to squirt cold viruses up their noses and monitor their responses. No, he wasn't a sadist, just a researcher.

"**Y**ou can lade a man up to th' university, but ye can't make him think."

—*Finley Peter Dunne*

One famous Ball State University graduate gives students up to $10,000 for having average grades, simply because he also had had average grades while attending there. The plaque, dedicated to the scholarship program reads, "Dedicated to All C-Students Before Me and After Me—David Letterman."

"The C students run the world."

—Harry Truman

The T.W.I.N.K.I.E.S. Project (Tests With Inorganic Noxious Kakes In Extreme Situations) was carried out in 1995 at Rice University by a group of students during finals week. The "project" boiled down to the students subjecting Twinkie snack cakes to all sorts of experiments, from radiation and gravity to flames and heat. Despite the absurdity of it all, the subsequent Web site has been a favorite for junior high and high school science teachers ever since: http://www.twinkiesproject. com/.

Some things an education just can't fix: Evan Hansen, a student at Brigham Young University in Salt Lake City, Utah, entered a radio contest called "the most outrageous stunt." Hansen sawed off the roof of his car, filled it with a thousand pounds of raspberry Jell-O and 16 gallons of whipped cream, and won $500. He then drove to a shopping mall and dumped the sticky, gooey mess down a storm drain. Unfortunately, he was fined $500 for violating Utah's Water Pollution Control Act.

"University politics are vicious precisely because the stakes are so small."

—Henry Kissinger

Your University Dollars Hard at Work: University of Pittsburgh conducted tests on smell and gender. They lined up students and had them smell exhaled air and then guess if it had been blown by a male or a female. Nineteen out of twenty students guessed the correct gender by breath-smell alone.

Steve Jobs and Steve Wozniak, inventors of the Apple computer, were cooking up electronic money-making schemes long before they created their Apple empire. While Wozniak was a student at the University of California at Berkeley and

Jobs was still in high school, the two concocted the "blue box." With the help of Jobs getting the supplies, Wozniak created the box, which allowed them to tap into AT&T phone lines and make free long distance calls. They sold additional units to other students for $150 each.

"**A** man who has never gone to school may steal from a freight car; but if he has a university education he may steal the whole railroad."

—*Theodore Roosevelt*

Your Education Dollars at Work: A professor of biology at Southeastern Louisiana University once conducted a test about road kill. By placing rubber animals in the road or alongside the road and surveying over 20,000 motorists, he came to the conclusion that very few animals turned into road kill by accident—many swerved to deliberately hit the rubber decoys.

When Andrew Martinez began going to classes nude in 1992, there were no rules on the books at the University of California, Berkeley, that prevented it. As a matter of fact, the school did nothing until complaints began rolling in. In response to the ruckus, they added a new rule.

"My degree was a kind of inoculation. I got just enough education to make me immune from it for the rest of my life."

—*Alan Bennett*

thirteen

Worldly Wise

In the world, there are 100 million children who never go to school.

In a poor country, one year of schooling is worth 10 percent to 20 percent increased income for life, every year.

In the developing country of Brazil, the government pays mothers in poor families if they send their kids to school. About 30 percent of all Brazilian families are eligible. Once a month, the mom gets a certificate from school if her child was there at least 85 percent of the time. At the local lottery office, the certificate and ID card are all she needs to show to get cash on the spot. The system works pretty well—at last count, 97 percent of Brazil's kids are in school.

The world's biggest high school is Rizal High School in Manila, Philippines. The student body at last count numbered 19,738.

What's the only state with only one school district? Hawaii.

Many Greenland schools teach fur sewing.

Out of all the Canadian provinces, the Yukon province has the highest average education level.

Islamic law requires that both boys and girls receive an education. Individual governments, however, don't always place this particular law at the top of their list of priorities, as is evidenced by some Islamic countries' high rate of illiteracy among their female populations.

The song "School's Out" by Alice Cooper was once banned by the apartheid South African government because it was being used as a protest song by black school kids.

fourteen

The Wild World of School Sports

"Go in to win. Don't admit defeat before you start."

—Woodrow Wilson to his football team, showing that pep talks haven't changed much over more than a century

You know that old playground standard "Tug of War"? It was an actual Olympic event from 1900 to 1920.

It was a physical education teacher who invented the game of basketball. In 1891, Canadian James Naismith was working at the YMCA in Springfield, Massachusetts, in the days when it saw itself as a school for clean living. His students were complaining about the winter regimen of indoor marching, gymnastics, and calisthenics. The chairman of the physical education department suggested Naismith come up with a game that could be played in a gymnasium. His only stipulations were that all players should have an equal chance to make plays, but without body contact or a heavy ball that could do damage to the players or gymnasium.

Basketball was almost called "boxball." That's what James Naismith asked the custodian to find for him as goals for his new game. The custodian couldn't find any sturdy wooden boxes, but offered a couple of empty half-bushel peach baskets. "That'll have to do," said Naismith.

Rugby was invented accidentally by a lad at Rugby School in Warwickshire, England. During a soccer game in 1823, William Ellis, frustrated by his team's low score, caught the ball and ran with it down the field. He was penalized and his captain apologized profusely, but some players decided to take the ball and run with it, coming up with a chaotic game they called "the Rugby game" or "Rugby football."

Rugby School, by the way, was also the school in the classic book, *Tom Brown's School Days.*

The students at McGill University in Montreal were instrumental in introducing the "egg-shaped" ball (as Harvard students called it) to early American football.

McGill students also helped invent hockey. They adopted a winter game invented by cold, bored British soldiers stationed nearby, and went about improving and codifying it.

Nowadays, football seems more important than academics at some schools. However, it wasn't always that way. For example, New Haven forbade Yale students from playing football and soccer in public parks in the 1800s.

"I will not permit 30 men to travel 400 miles merely to agitate a bag of wind," sniffed Andrew White, president of Cornell University, as he forbid Cornell's first planned intercollegiate football game in 1873, with the University of Michigan.

Football was nearly banned from college campuses in 1909 because so many players were being killed—twenty-seven in that year and hundreds more seriously injured. Even boxer John L. Sullivan, no stranger to brutal sports, observed "There's murder in that game!" after watching a Harvard-Yale game.

Wrote gunfighter-turned-sportswriter Bat Masterson, another man who didn't flinch easily from a little violence:

> Football is not a sport in any sense. It is a brutal and savage slugging match between two reckless opposing crowds. The rougher it is and the more killed and crippled, the more delighted are the spectators, who howl their heads off at the sight of a player stretched prone and unconscious on the hard and frozen ground.

Finally, an Intercollegiate Football Rules Committee was formed under the leadership of the president of Princeton, Woodrow Wilson (later president of the United States). Wilson actually knew something about the game, having coached a football team while a history professor at Wesleyan University in the 1880s.

The Football Rules Committee came up with rules to make the game less lethal, requiring helmets and prohibiting diving tackles, linked arms on offense, the lifting and carrying of ball carriers, and interference with pass receivers. Most people supported the changes, but many hardcore fans complained that the IFRC ruined the game forever.

The cult of the school sports hero didn't emerge until after World War I. During the 1920s, college stadiums were built and pep rallies emerged as a new art form. College recruiters were given unlimited budgets to offer prospective players not just free room, board, and (nominal) education, but also pocket money, post-graduation jobs, and sports cars.

"Gentlemen, you are about to play Harvard. You may never again do anything as important."

—*Yale coach Tad Jones, 1924*

The name of the first "bowl" games came from the "Yale Bowl," a round bowl-shaped stadium built in 1914.

Does the red-and-white uniform of Cornell University's football team make you hungry? They should—they're what inspired the guy who designed the Campbell's soup can.

Go Eagles! That's the most popular name for high school sports teams. Second most popular is "Lions."

NCAA college football teams with "cat" nicknames—Lions, Tigers, Cougars — outnumber those with "dog" nicknames—Bulldogs, Huskies, Terriers—by more than 2 to 1.

The all-male Ivy League Eight were, and still are: Brown, Columbia, Cornell, Dartmouth, Harvard, the University of Pennsylvania, Princeton, and Yale.

Although these eight schools had been playing sports against one another for many years prior, the phrase "Ivy League" wasn't coined until the mid-1930s, by sportswriter Caswell Adams. In a letter to Charles Funk, author of the book *Heavens to Betsy*, Adams wrote about how he came up with the term: "If I remember correctly, it was when Fordham's football team was riding high and playing big-name teams from all over the country. One afternoon mention in the office was made of Columbia and Princeton and the like and I, with complete humorous disparagement in mind, said, 'Oh, they're just Ivy League.' Stanley Woodward, then sports editor of the *New York Herald Tribune* picked up the phrase the next day and credited me with it."

It was a student—a divinity student at Yale named Amos Alonza Stagg—who created the first-ever tackling dummy for a football team.

A professor of medicine and physiology at the University of Florida—Dr. Robert Cade—invented the sports drink Gatorade, based on the amount of salt and liquids the body excreted during exercise. The drink was tested on the university's football team—the 'Gators—initially to see if Dr. Cade had come up with a good batch of sports aid. "Gator" ade was so successful it took off commercially within two years of those initial tests.

fifteen

Truer Words Were Never Spoken

"Twenty years of schoolin'
And they put you on the day shift."

—Bob Dylan

"The highest result of education is tolerance."

—Helen Keller

"There is no education like adversity."

—Benjamin Disraeli

"Knowledge—that is, education in its true sense—is our best protection against unreasoning prejudice and panic-making fear, whether engendered by special interest, illiberal minorities, or panic-stricken leaders."

—Franklin D. Roosevelt

"**A**n investment in knowledge always pays the best interest."

—*Benjamin Franklin*

"**T**he fate of empires depends on the education of youth."

—*Aristotle*

"**K**nowledge is power."

—*Francis Bacon*

"**H**e that increaseth knowledge increaseth sorrow."

—*Ecclesiastes*

"**T**he secret of education lies in respecting the pupil."

—*Ralph Waldo Emerson*

"The roots of education are bitter, but the fruit is sweet."

—Aristotle

"Soap and education are not as sudden as a massacre, but they are more deadly in the long run."

—Mark Twain

Aristotle was once asked to explain how superior an educated man was to an uneducated one. His answer was simple: "As much as the living are to the dead."

"No man who worships education has got the best out of education. Without a gentle contempt for education no man's education is complete."

—G. K. Chesterton

"The one real object of education is to leave a man in the condition of continually asking questions."

—Bishop Creighton

"If you think education is expensive, try ignorance."

—Derek Bok

"We should take care not to make the intellect our God; it has, of course, powerful muscles, but no personality."

—Albert Einstein

"An educated man is one who can entertain a new idea, entertain another person, and entertain himself."

—Sydney Wood

"Tim was so learned that he could name a horse in nine languages; so ignorant that he bought a cow to ride on."

—Benjamin Franklin in Poor Richard's Almanac

Education Is . . .

"Education is one of the few things a person is willing to pay for and not get."

—William Lowe Bryan

"Education is hanging around until you've caught on."

—Robert Frost

"Education is one of the chief obstacles to intelligence and freedom of thought."

—Bertrand Russell

"Education is a form of self-delusion."

—Elbert Hubbard

"Education is a process which makes a rogue cleverer than another."

—Oscar Wilde

"Education is the inculcation of the incomprehensible into the ignorant by the incompetent."

—Josiah Stamp

"Education consists mainly in what we have unlearned."

—Mark Twain

"Education is a succession of eye-openers each involving the repudiation of some previously held belief."

—George Bernard Shaw

"**E**ducation is what remains when we have forgotten all that we have been taught."

—George Savile

"**E**ducation has produced a vast population able to read but unable to distinguish what is worth reading."

—G. M. Trevelyan

"**E**ducation seems to be in America the only commodity of which the customer tried to get as little he can for his money."

—Max Forman

"**E**ducation is that which discloses to the wise and disguises from the foolish their lack of understanding."

—Ambrose Bierce

"**E**ducation should be gentle and stern, not cold and lax."

—*Joseph Joubert*

"**E**ducation is not filling a bucket, but lighting a fire."

—*William Yeats*

"**E**ducation is a weapon whose effect depends on who holds it in his hands and at whom it is aimed."

—*Joseph Stalin*

"**E**ducation is the process of casting false pearls before real swine."

—*Irwin Edman*

"Education is our passport to the future, for tomorrow belongs to the people who prepare for it today."

—*Malcolm X*

sixteen

Teachers on Page, Stage, and Screen

M*wah-mwah, mwah mwah mwah mwah:* Although there were several teachers that appeared, by name, in the *Peanuts* cartoons, only one was specifically noted to be Charlie Brown's. Her name was Mrs. Donovan.

Call Me Ishmael: The lead character of Melville's classic *Moby Dick,* you'll remember, was a whaler. You may not remember, however, that he first gave up his job as a schoolmaster in Massachusetts to follow his heart and live on the sea.

The Scarecrow, one of Batman's nemeses, had been teacher Jonathan Crane before trading in his ruler and chalk for evil.

Miss Landers was the name of the Beave's schoolteacher on the TV show *Leave It to Beaver.*

The Prime of Miss Jean Brodie was a novel about a determined Scottish schoolteacher hellbent on turning the girls in her care into the *crème de la crème* of the school. Actress Maggie Smith *(Harry Potter and the Sorcerer's Stone, Tea with Mussolini,* and *Sister Act)* won an Oscar for her portrayal of Miss Jean Brodie in the 1969 movie.

A little trivia: In the '70s hit *Welcome Back Kotter,* Mr. Kotter's classroom was number 11. Not to be confused with *Room 222,* an earlier teacher drama/sitcom.

The ill-fated schoolteacher in the quaint little school in Hitchcock's *The Birds*? She was played by a young Suzanne Pleshette.

Barbie the doll has had two educational careers in the dozens of jobs she has worked. In 1965 she debuted as an elementary school teacher. In 1984, during American cultural decline, she taught aerobics.

Some of our favorite movies about educators include *Stand and Deliver, To Sir with Love, Goodbye Mr. Chips, Dead Poets Society, Matilda, Educating Rita, Lean on Me,* and *Harry Potter and the Sorcerer's Stone.*

The first movie about high school classes from hell was *Blackboard Jungle.* Starring Glenn Ford as teacher Richard Dadier, this 1950s movie is about taming an urban classroom of hooligans.

It was a school science fair project that turned Peter Parker into Spiderman. (A radioactive spider bit him.)

Never Trust a Man Who Can Do the Numbers: James Moriarty, the diabolical genius who was Sherlock Holmes' nemesis, worked as a mathematics professor when he wasn't doing other kinds of evil.

Arthur Conan Doyle's inspiration for Sherlock Holmes was a professor. While a medical student, Doyle was impressed by surgeon Dr. Joseph Bell, who could deduce such things as a patient's birthplace, class, military service, career, and travels merely by paying close attention to subtleties like accents, calluses on hands, and the way the person walked. When Doyle began writing fiction, he based his famous detective on Bell's personality and talents.

"Mary Had a Little Lamb" was inspired by a real-life occurrence in Sterling, Massachusetts, involving a girl named Mary Sawyer and her pet lamb who followed her to school. However, the actual authorship of the poem is a subject of controversy. Hometown folks say it was a classmate of Mary's named John Roulston who wrote the first verse, and that Sarah Hale (the woman who is generally credited with authorship) stole the famous first verse and added a more obscure last verse but took credit for the whole thing.

seventeen

An Alternative Education

The first known circus school opened in China during the T'ang Dynasty (612–907 A.D.). The curriculum included rope walking, long pole tricks, duel sword dancing, and seven ball jumping.

Want to teach advanced driver's training? Rolls Royce runs a school for chauffeurs.

You Can Easily Bull Your Way Through This Curriculum: California is home to the only matador school in the United States.

Until the 1880s, almost every barber in the United States was an African American. However, when barber schools opened in the 1880s, the father-to-son apprenticeship was broken, and whites entered the field in large numbers.

The first corporate university was McDonald's Hamburger University, opened in 1961 to ensure that McDonald's managers worldwide are as uniform as their hamburgers are.

Since then, more than 65,000 McDonald's managers have graduated from ol' Hamburger U. Besides the main campus in Oak Brook, Illinois, Hamburger Universities have opened in ten international locations including England, Japan, Germany, and Australia.

Ben and Jerry learned how to make ice cream from a $5 correspondence course in ice cream making from Pennsylvania State University.

Looking for a one-year sabbatical idea? Apply to drive the Oscar Meyer Weiner-mobile through the country—each year the company selects college graduates with backgrounds in public relations or teaching and sends them to Hot Dog High School in Madison, Wisconsin, to learn the basics of roadside public relations (and operating the vehicle itself). The teams drive off for a year in teams of two to make appearances throughout eight regions of the country. The bad news is that it's harder to get into Hot Dog High School than Harvard. Of the thousand of applicants each year, only sixteen are chosen.

eighteen

Lunches, Libraries, and Bus Drivers

Check out your school library. You might begin wondering, as we all have, who invented the Dewey Decimal System, the numbering system that classifies books by subject. No, not educator John Dewey, not Donald Duck's nephew, and not perennial presidential candidate Thomas Dewey. It was Melvil Dewey, an educator and librarian of the 1800s.

Melvil Dewey had a really good year in 1876. He not only published his Dewey Decimal Classification System, but he also helped found the American Library Association and the *Library Journal.*

Keep an eye on the support staff—remember that Lee Harvey Oswald worked in the Dallas warehouse for schoolbooks and supplies from which JFK was shot.

Living Off the Fat of the Land: The most popular school lunches are pizza, chicken nuggets, tacos, burritos, and hamburgers.

Ask the lunch servers if you want to, but studies show that boys drink more milk per capita than girls at school.

The all-time favorite school lunchbox of all time? The round-top school bus with Disney cartoon characters in every window. Nine million of them sold from 1961 to 1973.

The students at Boulder University are known for their morbid fascination with the local story of Alferd Packer and his cannibal monstrosities of the 1870s. Fifty years after Packer's conviction, the university students voted to rename the school cafeteria "Alferd Packer Memorial Grill." It serves the usual standards including some with unusual names, like the most popular dish, the "El Canibal" burrito.

The Wheels on the Bus Go 'Round and 'Round

Schools didn't start providing transportation for students until the late 1800s. By 1910, based on the premise that moving kids was cheaper than building new schools, thirty states were providing rides to and from schools.

Not that students were seeing yellow school buses coming down the street. More likely a horse-drawn hay wagon that had been hired from a local farmer.

Later, as gasoline-powered vehicles became more common, the "school wagon" was replaced with a "school truck."

It wasn't until the 1920s and '30s that school buses gradually became the standard for student transportation.

There are currently 440,000 public school buses on the road, transporting 23.5 million students a total of 4.3 billion miles a year.

About 4 percent of the annual cost of educating the average student goes toward transportation to and from school—a total of $493.

Don't underestimate the power of those who pay for them—it's the reason why only a few of the states mandate seat belts in school buses despite the support of a solid majority of voters and nearly all pediatrics associations. Waiting for action from the federal government? Forget it.

Do seatbelts save lives? Anti-seatbelt organizations trot out the same discredited arguments used by the auto companies in the 1960s to argue against mandatory seat belts in cars: Seatbelts will actually cause injuries, nobody will use them, they'll increase the chance of becoming "trapped" in an accident.

Anti-seatbelt groups out there straight-facedly brandish statistics that purportedly show that a child is "hundreds of times" safer unbelted in a school bus than belted in a family sedan. Advocates on the other side say that an unbelted child is many times *less* safe. Who to believe? Stay tuned, the few states that mandate seatbelts should be able to give some real-life data soon.

For the record, school buses are painted "chrome yellow." They used to be "Omaha orange."

Gas mileage for the average school bus? Seven miles per gallon.

Acknowledgments

The authors wish to thank their patient and understanding editor Leslie Berriman. Thanks to the following people, as well, all of whom have been invaluable during this project: Heather McArthur, Pam Suwinsky, Brenda Knight, Claudia Smelser, Jill Rogers, Jan Johnson, Jackson Hamner, Georgia Hamner, and Elana Mingo. The authors would also like to extend a special thank you to all of the teachers who took the time to help us in our research (specifically Laura Barrett and Deborah Newler). All of you deserve a lifetime of chocolate, money, and lattes, not necessarily in that order.

Selected References

Books

The Book of Answers: The New York Public Library Telephone Reference Service's Most Unusual and Entertaining Questions, by Barbara Berliner with Melinda Corey and George Ochoa. Fireside Books, 1990.

The Compact Edition of the Oxford English Dictionary. Oxford University Press, 1985.

Encyclopaedia Britannica, edited by the faculties of the University of Chicago. Benton Publishing, 1979.

The Guinness Book of Records: 1999, by Guinness Publishing Ltd. Bantam Books, 1999.

How in the World? by the editors of *Reader's Digest.* The Reader's Digest Association, Inc., 1990.

The Juicy Parts: Things Your History Teacher Never Told You about the 20th Century's Most Famous People, by Jack Mingo. Perigee Books, 1996.

Just Curious, Jeeves, by Jack Mingo and Erin Barrett. Ask Jeeves, Inc., 2000.

Just Curious about History, Jeeves, by Erin Barrett and Jack Mingo. Pocket Books, 2002.

News from the Fringe: True Stories of Weird People and Weirder Times, compiled by John J. Kohut and Roland Sweet. Plume Books, 1993.

The Origins of Everyday Things, by the editors of *Reader's Digest.* The Reader's Digest Association, Inc., 1999.

The Oxford Dictionary of Quotations, Third Edition, by Book Club Associates. Oxford University Press, 1980.

Panati's Extraordinary Origins of Everyday Things, by Charles Panati. Harper & Row Publishing, 1987.

Peter's Quotations: Ideas for Our Time from Socrates to Yogi Berra, Gems of Brevity, Wisdom, and Outrageous Wit, by Dr. Laurence J. Peter. William Morrow and Company, Inc., 1977.

Prime Time Proverbs: The Book of TV Quotes, by Jack Mingo and John Javna. Harmony Books, 1989.

School: The Story of American Public Education (The companion volume to the four-part PBS television series), edited by Sarah Mondale and Sarah B. Patton. Beacon Press, 2001.

Stories Behind Everyday Things, by the editors of *Reader's Digest.* The Reader's Digest Association, Inc., 1980.

The 2,548 Best Things Anybody Ever Said, by Robert Byrne. Galahad Books, 1996.

Uncle John's Bathroom Reader, by The Bathroom Readers Institute, Volumes I through XIII.

An Underground Education, by Richard Zacks. Anchor Books, 1997.

Webster's New World Dictionary, Third College Edition. Simon & Schuster, Inc., 1988.

Webster's Unabridged Dictionary, Second Edition. William Collins & World Publishing Co., Inc., 1976.

Weird History 101, by John Richard Stephens. Adams Media Corporation, 1997.

Why in the World? by the editors of *Reader's Digest.* The Reader's Digest Association, Inc., 1994.

Software

Microsoft *Encarta 98 Encyclopedia.* Microsoft 1997.

World Book Encyclopedia. IBM 1998.

Web Sites

Prof. Robert N. Barger's History of American Education, http://www.nd.edu/~rbarger/www7/

The Bureau of Labor Statistics, http://www.bls.org/; http://www.bls.gov/

Electric Library, http://www.elibrary.com/

The National Education Association, http://www.nea.org/

The National PTA, http://www.pta.org/

Urban Legends Reference Page, http://www.snopes2.com/

Useless Information, http://home.nycap.rr.com/useless/contents.html

About the Authors

Jen Fariello

Erin Barrett and Jack Mingo have authored twenty books, including *How the Cadillac Got Its Fins, The Couch Potato Guide to Life*, and the bestselling *Just Curious, Jeeves.* They write their own syndicated fun facts column, and have written articles for many major periodicals, including *Salon, The New York Times, The Washington Post,* and *Reader's Digest* and generated more than 30,000 questions for trivia games. From their home in the San Francisco Bay Area, they're main homework assignment is teaching their children how to be first rate know-it-alls.

You can contact Erin and Jack at:
ErinBarrett@sbcglobal.net
JackMingo@sbcglobal.net